Praise for

Our Secret Paradise

Filled with straightforward truths and practical applications, *Our Secret Paradise* will empower and encourage your marriage. If you need insight, healing or even a rekindled fire in your marriage, this book will guide you to the place God has promised for you and your spouse. *Our Secret Paradise* is a must-read for those who long for God's absolute best in their marriage.

John Bevere

AUTHOR, *THE BAIT OF SATAN*, *THE FEAR OF THE LORD* AND *UNDER COVER*
FOUNDER, JOHN BEVERE MINISTRIES

Jimmy Evans has masterfully coupled Scripture, personal experience and godly wisdom to create a refreshing and insightful manual on building powerful marriages! This book will most assuredly make good marriages even better. Put on your seatbelts—things are going to change in your house.

Dr. John C. Hagee

PASTOR, CORNERSTONE CHURCH

Jimmy and Karen Evans have a God-given passion to help couples of all ages. We've seen their work up close and personal—we know their hearts. In *Our Secret Paradise*, Jimmy brings a message of optimistic fervor for restoring marriage to everything God intended it to be.

Drs. Les and Leslie Parrott

AUTHORS, *LOVE TALK*
FOUNDERS, CENTER FOR RELATIONSHIP DEVELOPMENT

our secret
paradise

JIMMY EVANS

Regal

From Gospel Light
Ventura, California, U.S.A.

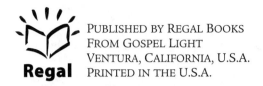

PUBLISHED BY REGAL BOOKS
FROM GOSPEL LIGHT
VENTURA, CALIFORNIA, U.S.A.
PRINTED IN THE U.S.A.

Regal Books is a ministry of Gospel Light, a Christian publisher dedicated to serving the local church. We believe God's vision for Gospel Light is to provide church leaders with biblical, user-friendly materials that will help them evangelize, disciple and minister to children, youth and families.

It is our prayer that this Regal book will help you discover biblical truth for your own life and help you meet the needs of others. May God richly bless you.

For a free catalog of resources from Regal Books/Gospel Light, please call your Christian supplier or contact us at 1-800-4-GOSPEL or www.regalbooks.com.

Library of Congress Cataloging-in-Publication Data
Evans, Jimmy.
  Our secret paradise / Jimmy Evans.
    p. cm.
  ISBN 0-8307-3904-1 (hard cover) — ISBN 0-8307-3906-8 (international trade paper)
  1. Marriage—Religious aspects—Christianity. I. Title.
  BV835.E885 2006
  248.8'44—dc22   2006003018

1   2   3   4   5   6   7   8   9   10   /   10   09   08   07   06

Rights for publishing this book in other languages are contracted by Gospel Light Worldwide, the international nonprofit ministry of Gospel Light. Gospel Light Worldwide also provides publishing and technical assistance to international publishers dedicated to producing Sunday School and Vacation Bible School curricula and books in the languages of the world. For additional information, visit www.gospellightworldwide.org; write to Gospel Light Worldwide, P.O. Box 3875, Ventura, CA 93006; or send an e-mail to info@gospellightworldwide.org.

Dedication

I dedicate this book to the love of my life, Karen,
who has truly made my life a paradise with her beauty,
joy and friendship. I also include in this dedication our
twin granddaughters, Abby and Elle. I pray that they and
their generations will experience a legacy of love
and success in marriage.

Contents

Secret One
Triumphant Realism

Secret Two
A Redemptive Spirit

Secret Three
A Passion That Lasts

Secret Seven
Prayer, Partnership and Purpose

Foreword

Have you ever met a couple that you immediately sensed were the type you would want to spend time with, learn from and lift up their arms, as Aaron did for Moses, as you watch God use them to His fullest desire? That is what Barb and I felt when we met Jimmy and Karen Evans.

I had seen them on television several times but was somewhat unfamiliar with their ministry, and I commented to Barb, "I like these two. They are genuine, biblical, and they have a great message for marriages today. And they really seem to love each other!"

Months later, we had the opportunity to join Jimmy and Karen for dinner, and an immediate friendship was built. Since that time, we have joined them on their television show, they have joined us on our radio program, and we have shared meals, laughter, grand-parenting stories and dreams for strong marriages in America and beyond. Our hearts are beating for the same thing—the hope for strong marriages in the midst of a culture that is not friendly toward marriage.

Jimmy and Karen are the real deal, whether they are standing on a platform speaking, hosting a television program or sitting down over a meal. They are passionate about marriages; their own marriage and the marriages of those they serve, including yours. As you read *Our Secret Paradise*, you will find that Jimmy and Karen bring their hearts and their experiences to each and every page. This book is biblical, practical and full of rich illustrations of the Evans's home and marriage. They are open about their own hearts and their experiences, not painting a picture of perfection but rather one of being sold out to help marriages grow that are on their watch.

The seven secrets—the foundational principles to a better marriage—will give you hope. If you are single and discouraged about the potential for a healthy biblical marriage, Jimmy and Karen will paint a picture of what it takes to have a great marriage and encourage you to seek God's best for yourself. If you are currently married and struggling, this book will give you a road map so that you can make midcourse corrections to recapture your own secret paradise. And if you are concerned about the state of marriage in general, your hearts will ring along with Jimmy and Karen's. They are sounding a clarion call for the Church and for those of us who are passionate about the restoration of God's institution of marriage. Real marriage. Biblical marriage.

As you read and discuss these secrets with your spouse, be prepared to open your hearts to the Lord so that He can do the work within you as well as in your marriage. Jimmy and Karen unpack great insights into the importance of healing and forgiveness, building friendship in marriage, vibrant sexual intimacy in marriage and more. We encourage you to read each section, share with your spouse what you are learning, and open your heart to what your spouse is learning. Pray together over the sections as God leads you. And when you finish this great book, share it with a couple you care about. They will thank you for it.

Dr. Gary and Barb Rosberg
America's Family Coaches
Co-authors, *Five Love Needs of Men and Women*
and *DivorceProof Your Marriage*
Co-hosts, *America's Family Coaches . . . LIVE!* daily radio program

Opening Word

We watch daytime soap operas and take vacations on remote tropical islands, looking for paradise. But the more we embrace these fantasies, the farther away paradise seems. The reason for our disappointment is that these dream worlds, of course, are not reality. Like so much that we see on television, in chick flicks and in romance novels today, they are imitations—or at best, temporary escapes. Dream as we may, these fantasies cannot satisfy the deepest longings in our hearts. Only God can do that.

Does this mean that we give up on the idea of paradise? Absolutely not. In fact, I can tell you that paradise in life—and specifically in marriage—is possible.

Jimmy and I have taken revelations of truth and applied them to our marriage for more than 25 years. Sometimes we could not see the benefits, but he and I continued to have faith in the Lord, who gives us the power to apply that truth in our everyday lives. I am so grateful to be married to a covenant-keeping husband who continues to believe and will not stop loving me.

The blessings in our lives have come because of our faith and perseverance in believing that a covenant-keeping God would lead us through the times in our marriage that were anything but paradise. I want to encourage you to read this book knowing that not only do we know and understand hopelessness, but also that we truly now live in a secret paradise. I am so thankful to Jimmy for all the truth he continues to apply that provides me with a very loving and secure marriage.

Jimmy and I experienced the proof of this truth this past December. We took a trip to one of those remote islands, not looking for paradise, but just needing rest. Having taken many great trips, this one was truly our best one ever. One morning after our quiet time, we were sharing our hearts with each other and we both realized that even though we were staying in a place of paradise, the greatest blessing was enjoying it at a time when our marriage was reaping the benefits of applying these principles.

I want to encourage you to begin today doing what Jimmy is writing about in this book. As your marriage blossoms into your own secret paradise, be reminded that all things can become new. I am blessed to be married to a man who provides an awesome paradise for me. I love you, Jimmy! Thank you for believing in us. Thank you for never giving up. It has all been worth it.

Love,

Karen Evans

Introduction

Paradise.

The word evokes powerful images and emotions. Oceans, mountains, meadows. Happiness, tranquility, satisfaction. Romance. We envision paradise as white-sand beaches, lush flora-draped atolls and hand-woven hammocks that sway between palm trees. We think Hawaii, Tahiti, the Bahamas. (Sometimes I think Gilligan's Island—after all, how bad can a place be when you have a guy with you who can build a microwave oven out of coconut shells, twine and a coat hanger!)

Paradise.

We picture Rocky Mountain vistas, clear brooks that gently wind through rambling meadows of Aspen daisies and a night sky ablaze with all of the stars in the universe. (In my picture I include a manicured golf course within walking distance, but that's just me.)

Add romance to the mix, and our minds effortlessly shift into overdrive. We sing songs, write poetry, read books and watch movies about it. (Go ahead—admit that you know the words to "Two Tickets to Paradise." I do!)

Paradise. We like the idea. We want to go there. We want to stay there.

When thinking about this heaven on Earth, our minds easily drift to the Garden of Eden. Even people who have never gone to church or read a single verse of the Bible know about Adam and Eve and the place where they once lived. The Garden of Eden was the original paradise, not only because of its spectacular, flawless setting but also because of the unspoiled rapport enjoyed there between the first husband and the first wife. Adam and Eve's relationship indeed was as idyllic as their Garden habitat. They not only lived in paradise, but they also lived it out with one another. It was the way God designed marriage to be.

A Faded Dream

In one way or another, we all desire what Adam and Eve had before their infamous fall. Why wouldn't we? The very word "Eden" refers to a place of pleasure, delight and fulfillment. This is the stuff that all brides- and grooms-to-be dream about. Didn't you? I did!

Perhaps "paradise" isn't the first word that springs to your mind when you think about your marriage. Maybe you have a few other terms for it—but not that one!

I hear you. Be assured, you're not alone. Most American couples probably agree. In fact, there was a time when I felt the same way about my marriage. The simple reality is that today too many couples have settled for mere survival in marriage or have given up and joined the ranks of the divorced. In many quarters, paradise as a dream for marriage has almost faded to black.

This is not surprising given the world in which we live. The paradise of Eden was destroyed by the prideful, rebellious choices of Adam and Eve. When they fell, they took God's ideal plan for marriage down with them. Although this didn't mean that couples couldn't attain paradise, it sure made it much tougher. Look around the world in which we live. Even today, the evidence is everywhere.

As I write this book, the average age of men who marry for the first time is 27. Women typically wait until they are 25.[1] Most single people *want* to be married yet are terrified at the thought. And with good reason! More than half of all marriages end in failure. In fact, the divorce rate has hovered above the 50-percent mark for decades, which means that most people in their 20s have never known a time when staying married to the same person for a lifetime was the norm. That's pretty sobering. What's more, many husbands and wives fear that they are only one major incident away from ending their marriage in a heap.

This ambivalence runs rampant in our American culture. Signs pop up everywhere. Not long before I wrote this book, our *Marriage Today* camera crew went to a high school campus to videotape a segment for our television show. All of the students that the crew interviewed were apprehensive at the prospect of walking down the aisle. They feared failing at marriage. Moreover, they strongly suspected that a lifetime of happiness and fulfillment in a commitment to one person was simply impossible. These students were not in New York or San Francisco, where nonchalance toward marriage might be expected—they were just down the road from my old office in Amarillo, Texas!

Steadily we are bombarded by staggering divorce statistics, a less-than-marriage-friendly culture and our own shortcomings. With so many discouraging reports and such sweeping pessimism, should we jettison the idea of thriving and settle for mere survival in marriage? Should we give up on God's design for marital paradise?

FROM SURVIVING TO THRIVING

My wife, Karen, and I have experienced both surviving in marriage (barely) and thriving in it. Believe me, each of us knows what being in a bad marriage is like.

After three years of intense and, at times, troubled dating during high school, Karen and I married. At 19 years of age, neither of us had the slightest idea of the skills it would take to succeed as husband and wife, nor did we realize the dangers we would face. However, we knew that we loved one another, and we were determined to make a life together.

During our first three years of marriage, we resembled two parched people frantically trying to satisfy their thirsts in a desert. As most couples do, we married one another because we each believed the other could meet our needs and fulfill our desires. Our courtship had not been perfect or always peaceful, yet we believed that any problems we experienced could be solved if only we were married. So we jumped from the proverbial frying pan into the fire.

Our poor marriage preparation (overlaid with ignorance, immaturity and disappointment) brought us to a point in which many couples find themselves. By our fifth anniversary, we were out of love. Every year, we had fought with increasing frequency and intensity, becoming more numb and disillusioned with each quarrel. However, the darkest moments began when we both became convinced that our marriage had been a mistake. If only we had chosen the right person to marry, we would not have all of these problems—or so we reasoned.

I wish I could tell you that we got ourselves into that mess before we became Christians. Sadly, both of us were committed Christians when we married. Karen and I attended church each Sunday. We believed wholeheartedly in the Bible. Yet we were products of a society that requires years of training for almost any significant career endeavor but requires no significant preparation for the most crucial undertaking in life: marriage. We were racing toward marital ruin because we had not been taught how to function in the most important human relationship on Earth.

The final hurdle in our downward slide came one evening when we were having the same old fight about unmet needs and pet frustrations for what seemed the five-hundredth time. Karen repeatedly accused me of not loving her as much as I loved my job and of not meeting her needs. Finally, angry, hurt and defensive, I jumped to my feet, pointed a shaking finger toward our bedroom, and shouted, "Go pack your bags, and get out of this house and out of my life!"

As Karen ran out of the room sobbing, I sat down in my chair and stared at the blank television screen as if nothing had happened. Yet deep inside, my heart was torn in two. I didn't want her to leave, but I did not believe that I could take any more of the strife and contention if she stayed. That was one of the lowest points of my life and, without a doubt, the lowest point in our marriage.

Meanwhile, Karen was crying in the bedroom. She felt the same as I did. She cared deeply for me and cherished many of the memories of our life together. Yet she had endured so much suffering in the marriage that she had now lost much of her respect—and much of her affection—for me.

I began to rehearse what I would do (and what she probably would do) if we split up. The more I thought about it, the more I hurt. I didn't want to lose Karen, but I didn't know how to keep her. Fortunately, at that moment something inside me broke. This was new for me and not typically the way I reacted to our quarrels. After a few moments of prayer and contemplation, I also began to embrace and yield to what God was trying to teach me.

As I yielded to God, I suddenly saw things in a different light. For the first time in my married life, I knew that I was wrong. For years, I had been unwilling to accept responsibility for any of the problems with our marriage. When Karen and I fought, I always found a way to make it look as if it were her fault. But that evening, I was overwhelmed with the reality that I didn't know how to be a husband. This awareness stood in stark contrast to the overbearing arrogance and chauvinism that had characterized my life up to that moment.

As the truth concerning our problems began to sink into my heart, I was reminded of a Scripture about the Holy Spirit, which I had read only weeks before:

> But the Counselor, the Holy Spirit, whom the Father will send in my name, will teach you all things and will remind you of everything I have said to you (John 14:26, *NIV*).

In that moment, as clearly as my own shortcomings were being exposed, the Lord spoke to my heart that He was the solution. Through His bringing of that Bible verse to my mind, I began to realize that He was present in my life to teach me all things. Those two words—"all things"—kept echoing through my mind until they finally sank in. If the Holy Spirit was sent to teach me all things, then He could even teach me how to be a husband!

Alone in the living room, I got out of my chair and fell to my knees. "Holy Spirit," I whispered, still choked with emotion, "Jesus said that He sent You to teach His followers all things. I am asking You to show me how to be a husband, because I don't know how, and no one has ever taught me. Please help me to learn to love Karen as I should. I am so sorry for all of the things I have done to damage our marriage and to hurt her. Please forgive me and help me. In Jesus' name, amen."

After my prayer, which I said in faith, I knew that something was happening within me. It was not some superglorious or spooky feeling. Nevertheless, something was changing deep inside me. At that moment, God began a work of bringing truth and humility into my heart. He began to prepare me to learn to look at marriage in a different light and to change not only my attitude but also my behavior. He simultaneously did a work in Karen, too. From that day forward, our marriage has grown progressively richer, fuller and more satisfying.

TWO TICKETS TO EDEN

Paradise. Is it really possible?

Several years ago, Rutgers University conducted a study in which they asked men and women across America about their attitudes regarding marriage. Ninety-three percent said that having a secure marriage for a lifetime was very important, but fewer than half thought such a relationship was possible for them personally.[2] In other words, the *dream* of a happy marriage has not died, but the *hope* in people's hearts that it can actually happen has disappeared.

That's why I have written this book. A marriage that thrives is not just a dream, a wish or a childhood fantasy. It's possible—here and now. In fact, believe it or not, it's actually how God intended every husband-and-wife relationship to be!

In the years since God turned my marriage around, He has shown Karen and me much about how to help others experience the same kind of transformation. God has used us to help thousands of couples make hurting marriages whole and good marriages even better.

What I share on the pages that follow are simple choices you can make and practical steps you can take to make your marriage the paradise God created it to be. So be encouraged. Be hopeful! In spite of where you are today in your marriage (or in a previous marriage), I want you to know that you have a loving and merciful God. There's nothing the devil has done to you that God can't undo. There's nothing that has been stolen from you that can't be restored. There's nothing that you have done to yourself that God won't forgive and heal.

Our Secret Paradise is a journey. Some of what you are about to read will challenge you. Some of it will be painful. That's why I also lighten up things by freely poking fun at myself. (I can assure you, in the early days of our marriage, my wonderful wife, Karen, and I made every bone-headed mistake humanly possible, so we're great examples!)

This is not a book about how to survive marriage. Mere survival is not an acceptable option, so let's dismiss that at the outset. Rather, this is a manual on how to build a marriage that thrives—a guide to matrimony in paradise. Every chapter of this book is designed to help you take hold of the triumphant reality that there is a secret paradise waiting for you and your spouse.

Jesus came to live on Earth, die and rise again to restore to us what was lost in Eden, and that includes the promise of a rock-solid marriage. When God came to restore the people whom He had created, He likewise restored the husband-and-wife relationship. I want to show you, as much as is possible in a fallen world, how we can go back to Eden. With this as the goal, I offer to you seven secrets that I believe can take you and your spouse to paradise. You can have a secure and satisfying marriage *for the rest of your life.*

Read and thrive!

Notes

1. *Population Profile of the United States: Living Together, Living Alone,* "Families and Living Arrangements," p. 52, November 8, 2005. *U.S. Census Bureau.* www.census.gov (accessed February 14, 2006).
2. Barbara Dafoe Whitehead and David Popenoe, *National Marriage Project, 1999, 2002. Rutgers University.* http://marriage.rutgers.edu (accessed February 14, 2006).

Triumphant Realism

Disappointment is a sort of bankruptcy—
the bankruptcy of a soul that expends too
much in hope and expectation.

Eric Hoffer (1902–1983), U.S. philosopher

CHAPTER 1

Broken Hearts

Back in the Garden of Eden, God said, "It is not good for the man to be alone" (Gen. 2:18). I can attest to the truth of that statement. Men *need* women. We're not much good without them. In fact, research shows that a 48-year-old married man has a 90 percent chance of reaching the age of 65, but a 48-year-old single man has only a 60 percent chance of reaching that age.[1] Obviously, God knew what He was talking about. It's not good for men to be alone—in fact, it's downright hazardous to their health! And contrary to what the popular culture tries to sell us these days, women need men, too. In God's divine order of things, men and women are much better together than alone.

Nevertheless, one of the great questions of our generation seems to be whether any couple can truly expect to have a lasting marriage. And, if so, how? It's not that people have stopped dreaming about a blissful, life-long relationship. They've just seen too many of those dreams end up as nightmares! But what causes those dreams to turn into nightmares? In my many years of counseling couples in crisis, I've discovered that it's not primarily problems with the checkbook or in the bedroom that is at the root of the trouble. Actually, the number one reason for divorce is *disappointment*.

I had a front-row seat as I watched disappointment do its destructive work in my own home. As I already noted, in the first three years of our marriage, Karen and I were both swamped by disappointment. For me, those early years were pretty much God bursting one unrealistic expectation and false assumption after another.

LEAVE FANTASY BEHIND

Most of us bring multiple layers of false expectations to our wedding day. We carry into our relationships Hollywood-painted fantasies of bliss and dreams of living happily ever after. When those expectations invariably prove to be fiction, we often find ourselves standing knee-deep in the shattered remnants of our dreams. Perhaps you've stood in that lonely, desolate spot.

This vulnerable moment is often the cue the devil has been waiting for to come in and tell us that we've made a mistake—that we've married the wrong person or that our true soul mate was the one behind door number 2. He'll whisper that we have to get out of this relationship or we'll be trapped in misery for the rest of our life!

This is why it is so crucial for us to understand that in order to be married successfully, we must approach the relationship with the right set of expectations. When we do, our chances for success increase enormously. If we don't, we may not be destined to fail, but we will certainly be destined for disappointment.

This is the root of the divorce epidemic in America today. Millions of married couples are prisoners of unrealistic expectations about what it takes to arrive at paradise. That's why our collective hope for secure and lasting relationships is dying. It's perishing one broken heart at a time. And in nearly every case, it is the result of marriages that were born in fantasy instead of grounded in reality. Why is this happening? One of the primary reasons is because of the way that we as a culture market marriage and "sell" ourselves to potential mates.

When we find someone that we think could be a good prospect, we suddenly turn into the greatest salesperson in the world! We think that the right way to win the attention and commitment of a potential mate is by showing off all of our good points, minimizing the bad ones, and—at all costs—hiding the worst ones. Then we glamorize the wedding ceremony as if it were something out of a fairy tale. After all, if a ceremony is beautiful enough, it will neutralize any post-honeymoon problems, right? Wrong!

Is this really good preparation for marriage? For that matter, is it good preparation for any type of meaningful relationship?

COUNT THE COST

It's enlightening to compare this process of recruiting a potential mate to Jesus' approach to recruiting His disciples:

> Great multitudes went with Him. And He turned and said to them, "If anyone comes to Me and does not hate his father and mother, wife and children, brothers and sisters, yes, and his own life also, he cannot be My disciple. And whoever does not bear his cross and come after Me cannot be My disciple. For which of you, intending to build a tower, does not sit down first and count the cost, whether he has enough to finish it—lest after he has laid the foundation, and is not able to finish, all who see it begin to mock him, saying, 'This man began to build and was not able to finish.' Or what king, going to make war against another king, does not sit down first and consider whether he is able with ten thousand to meet him who comes against him with twenty thousand? Or else, while the other is still a great way off, he sends a delegation and asks conditions of peace. So likewise, whoever of you who does not forsake all that he has cannot be My disciple" (Luke 14:25-33).

Perhaps you're thinking, *Wow, Jimmy, how can that Bible passage possibly relate to marriage? "To be a disciple, you are going to have to hate your mother, father, wife and children, brothers and sisters"? That doesn't exactly sound like a pro-family ministry to me!*

I have to agree that it certainly doesn't sound anything like the way Madison Avenue lures new customers, political candidates solicit voters, or the military entices new recruits. So why is Jesus' unorthodox approach the right way to impress a potential mate? Take a close look at what Jesus said. You'll see that His way is not only the right way—but that it is also the *only* way.

Although everyone who followed Christ ultimately discovered how truly wonderful life with Jesus was, He didn't attract followers with flowery speech. Nor did He try to talk people into a discipleship commitment by declaring all of His wonderful attributes. As we saw in the passage above, Jesus did just the opposite. Instead of painting the best possible outcome, He made would-be disciples consider the worst-case scenario. He had them count the cost before they even began.

Jesus dealt with the bad stuff right up front. He told those who wanted to follow Him that they would have to give up everything they had. In comparison to their commitment to Christ, they would have to "hate" their mother, father, wife, children, brothers and sisters. He told those who were thinking about following Him that the question they needed to settle before they went any farther was this: *Am I willing to pay the ultimate price to be in a relationship with Christ?*

What is the result of this let's-get-real approach to relationship? Jesus' disciples always know what they are getting into. The relationship is never less than He says it will be. Quite the opposite, the relationship with Jesus is always much more than anyone ever imagines. No disappointments. And because those who truly want to follow Christ have to deal with reality right up front, they never turn back or die of disappointment. All the surprises are pleasant ones.

Promising that everything is always going to be wonderful is not Jesus' way. But there *is* one who uses that tactic—it's the devil's primary recruitment strategy. He uses it to get us to go his way. Then, after we commit to his program, he always disappoints. It's the classic bait-and-switch tactic. That's precisely what he is doing in many marriages today.

REMEMBER YOUR VOWS

Marriage is a complex and important relationship that encompasses every area of life. Yet despite this fact, most couples get married with little or no preparation. They expect to succeed without ever having read a book on marriage or having attended a seminar—without ever having sought out any information at all. They give their marriage far less preparation than they would give any other life-changing event. I suspect most married people spend more hours on computer training than they do on developing their marriage and family skills.

This is not to say that most people totally dismiss the possibility that their future spouses will have needs and issues that will need to be fixed or healed. But instead of preparing for their part in that healing process, they expect the "magic" of the wedding to fix whatever is wrong. And that's a prescription for disappointment.

If the weddings that I've attended over the last decade are indicators, then old-fashioned, traditional vows have fallen out of favor. One popular wedding website offers 81 different choices of wedding vows, ranging from traditional to unconventional.[2] Can't find what you're looking for? Then follow one of the website's handy guides for creating your own!

The demise of the traditional vows coincides rather tightly with the rise in the divorce rate in this country. Coincidence? I don't think so! You see, the traditional wedding vows were plainly intended to put a couple that was getting married in touch with harsh reality.

For instance, do you remember that part in the vows in which the bride and groom promise to stick together through richer or poorer, for better or for worse, in sickness and in health? Right there in the marriage vows we have a reality session. The bride and groom say to each other, "Hey, you know something? I am getting married to you, and I am prepared for the worst. I do not want the worst, but I am prepared for the worst. I do not want to go through being poor, but if poorer comes, I am prepared for it. I'm not looking for sickness to come, but if it does, I am prepared to go through that with you, too." By founding their hopes on fantasy instead of facts, the modern bride and groom ignore what traditional wedding vows were plainly created to do—put the couple in touch with reality.

Even if these traditional vows are used, a deeply imbedded delusion often prevents most couples at the marriage altar from accepting the real blessing of their vows. Even as these couples repeat these vows, they think to themselves, *This is not going to happen to us. Yes, I know I am saying "for better or for worse," but our marriage is going to be nothing but "better." Yes, I noticed some things wrong with the other person—but I am just sure that God is going to fix those things during this ceremony. And besides, I believe I can straighten out anything that God doesn't fix pretty quickly after the ceremony.*

This is not reality. After the ceremony is over and the couple begins sharing their life together as one, their dream of marriage as a paradise is quickly assaulted by reality. The result is often bitter disappointment.

On this count, Karen and I can speak from experience. During the first several years of our marriage, I wrestled with deep disappointment. I had absurdly unrealistic expectations of what marriage would be, and when those expectations were shattered, it ripped my heart out. To be frank, Karen and I were on the brink of divorce, because I was convinced that I had made a mistake.

Not only had the devil convinced me that I had made a mistake by getting married, but he also constantly reminded me of the girl that I "should" have married. She was a girl that I dated off and on in high school—usually during those times when I was trying to be mean to Karen. (I told you I was a real piece of work!) The devil would come to me and say, "You know, you should have married that other girl instead." Of course, the devil was wrong. He is a pathological liar.

I am so glad that I married Karen. She was and is the very best person for me! But because of my disappointment at that time, I began to think, *I've made a terrible mistake. I've got to get rid of Karen in order to be happy. We need to divorce. I don't want to live without her, but I don't know how to live with her.*

And do you know what? Karen was thinking similar thoughts! She was being crushed by disappointment, too. But the truth is that we didn't make a mistake. We just got married with all the wrong expectations.

FOR RICHER OR POORER

There are going to be problems in marriage. There is going to be a price that we will have to pay when we get married. It's not going to be all sunshine and roses. In fact, sometimes it's going to be all thunderstorms and thorns! That's why those traditional vows say "for better or for worse." There is going to be some worse. That's why they say "for richer or for poorer." There is going to be some poorer—we will have times of financial need and crises in our lives. And that is why they say "in sickness and in health." Our bodies are going to change—count on it! We are not always going to look as good as we looked on our wedding day.

We need to enter marriage fully prepared for reality. Yet many of us have deeply imbedded false expectations and assumptions instead.

"Poor won't happen to me!"

"Worse won't happen to me!"

"Sickness won't happen to me!"

Yes, they will. Just get ready for it. If you don't, the poison of disappointment will begin to drain the life out of your marriage.

The story of Vietnam War P.O.W. Admiral Jim Stockdale illustrates the value of staring hard reality in the face, no matter the circumstances. Admiral Stockdale served as the highest-ranking officer in the infamous Hanoi Hilton prisoner-of-war camp from 1965 to 1973. While he was there, he suffered greatly at the hands of his captors. His story is one of not only personal survival but also of his mission to keep his men alive. He did save many of his men, but he also lost a few.[3]

When Admiral Stockdale was asked how he survived eight years in a prisoner of war camp, he replied, "I never lost faith in the end of the story. I never doubted that not only I would get out, but also that I would prevail in the end and turn the experience into a defining event in my life, which, in retrospect, I would not trade."[4]

When asked why some of his men didn't make it out, Admiral Stockdale explained that it was because these men were optimists: "They were the ones who said we're going to be out by Christmas, and Christmas would come and Christmas would go. They would say that we're going to be out by Easter, and Easter would come and Easter would go, and then Thanksgiving and then it would be Christmas again. They would die of a broken heart."

Comparing Admiral Stockdale's faith that he would *eventually* get out with the optimism of those who insisted they would *soon* get out, he says, "This is a very important lesson: You must never confuse faith that you will prevail in the end, (which you can never afford to lose), with the discipline to confront the most brutal facts of your current reality whatever they may be."

What Admiral Stockdale told his men to prepare them mentally to survive in a prisoner of war camp was, "You're not getting out by Christmas, but you will get out eventually. Now deal with that."

Most of the prisoners who believed him survived, and they are now walking around free in the United States of America. Many of the ones who did not believe him died of a broken heart in Vietnam. They never saw freedom again. It was not the conditions of their imprisonment that killed them; what took their lives were expectations based on fantasy rather than reality. The same principle applies to marriage, and the same expectations can be held. Expect your marriage to be perfect by Christmas, and you will fail. Face the reality of your circumstances, and expect it to be better eventually, and you will build up the faith to get there.

GET REAL

Here's the problem: We've been afraid to get real about marriage. Getting real does not mean giving up on the idea that marriage is designed to be the happiest and most meaningful relationship on Earth. What it does mean, however, is that to experience the paradise that marriage makes possible, we first have to recognize the deep needs that each of us as men and women carry into marriage. Only then will we begin to see the real romance of this nurturing, healing institution.

If we are not willing to get real about our marriages, we are in for a shock, because reality will eventually come and kick the door down. The fantasy can last for a while, but a day will come when our eyes will open to the fact that we and our spouses—and everyone else in the world—have real needs and issues to be dealt with. That's the day we wake up to reality. Go ahead, take that first stop along the path to paradise.

Notes
1. Linda Waite and Maggie Gallagher; *The Case for Marriage: Why Married People are Happier, Healthier, and Better Off Financially* (New York: Broadway Publishers, 2001), p. 49
2. "Inside the Guide: Vows," *The Ultimate Internet Wedding Guide.* http://www.ulti-matewedding.com (accessed October 11, 2005).
3. United States Naval Institute; Oral History Project; *Vietnam POW Interviews: Volume I.* http://www.usni.org/oralhistory/Collections/pow.htm (accessed February 2006).
4. James Stockdale, *Courage Under Fire: Testing Epictetus's Doctrines in a Laboratory of Human Behavior* (Hoover Institute, 1993), n.p.

CHAPTER 2

The Healing Journey

The photographs have been snapped, the bouquet has been tossed, and the reception is now over. As the wedding guests shower the happy couple with rice, the bride and groom climb into their limousine to begin their honeymoon—the start of their new lives together. The couple soon arrives at their destination and enters a special place in paradise—let's call it the Newlywed-Bliss Room. The surroundings are peaceful, the light is low and soft, and everything seems so lovely. The husband and the wife look great and behave so sweetly toward each other—so caring and loving.

Romance novels, bridal magazines and *The Bachelorette* TV show promise perpetual Newlywed Bliss. Too many of us believe the fairy tales and expect our marriages to be an immediate heaven on Earth. However, after just a few days, we must check out of the Newlywed-Bliss Room. That's when we wake up and get our first taste of marriage reality. Let's call this new place "Paradise Hospital." In Paradise Hospital, the husband and wife will look over at each other and see whom they have really married—*and start screaming* (at least on the inside). Now that is reality!

MESSED-UP MATES

We each have hurts from our past. We each have quirks in our personalities. No, I'm not referring only to our spouse—I'm talking about each of us! We all have areas of ignorance and we all deal with various levels of insecurity. We all have imbalances, wounds, scars and baggage that we carry around with us through life. This means that there is no one in the world whom we could marry who is not hurt, immature, imbalanced or ignorant, to at least a certain degree.

It's ironic, but some surveys (including the one conducted by Rutgers University) show that the reason people are so cautious about marriage today is that they are waiting to find their perfect "soul mate."[1] Popular culture has convinced people that if they wait long enough, they will unearth that certain person out there who will be "the one." Scores of books have been written and myriad websites launched to help people locate this elusive perfect match.

Let's visit the Reality Room for a moment: The truth is that this perfect person does not exist. Permit me to tell you something I know about your soul mate: He or she is deeply flawed! Women, I'm sorry I have to be the one to break the news, but your Prince Charming snores, makes the most insensitive remarks, and forgets anniversary dates. He's a mess. Men, your fantasy woman is moody, has irrational fears, and likes to shop. She's got issues.

There's no such thing as a person who is *not* messed up! Don't misunderstand, I'm not recommending that you just run out and marry the first dysfunctional person that you find. Single people, I encourage you to seek God's wisdom and marry a Christian person who shares your values, is compatible with your personality, and—of course—is attractive to you. But understand, when you find that person, he or she *will* be broken and hurting. You will have to face that person's personality quirks and emotional scars from his or her past. Regardless of how well that person behaves before the marriage, after the wedding you will see that person for who he or she really is—and it won't be pretty. So learn to deal with it!

Now, let me tell you the good news: When you go into marriage with your eyes open, you will be a good match for the person you do marry. Why? Because you're messed up too! If you are a mess, you can't marry someone who is perfect—it would be a mismatch. So face it—you, like everyone else, bear the wounds and scars of living in a fallen world filled with fallen people.

PARADISE HOSPITAL

When we look at marriage through the prism of reality, the quirks, hurts and insecurities that we see in the other person are not indications that we married the wrong person; rather, they are confirmations that we married the right one! I once heard someone say, "If both of you are the same, then one of you is unnecessary!" This is so true. The fact that we *are* so different is the very reason that we need each other.

When a couple discovers how different they are, they reach a crucial point. Instead of approaching these differences and needs correctly, many of us simply expect the differences to somehow just disappear. We hope that the wedding will magically fix everything so that we can dash off into paradise. No wonder most marriages fail.

If we want our marriage to be a paradise, then we must agree to stay awhile in Paradise Hospital. We have to get past the initial shock of waking up in sickbay (which many people don't get past). We need to realize that we need to accept our spouse's problems and accept the responsibility to be his or her healer. We have to understand that the wedding is actually the foyer to the hospital and that the ceremony is the first step on a journey of healing. Once we change how we see marriage, we will be on the road to finding paradise.

However exciting the idea of a journey sounds, the road to healing is definitely not what most people expect when they picture marriage. I'm sure that when standing at the altar very few couples think, *These are my first steps into a healing journey. Thank You, God, for giving me such a messed-up spouse so that we can start down this road together!* However, without exception, the husbands and wives who discover paradise in their marriages are the ones who have a willingness to be healers to their spouses and who allow their spouses to be healers to them. They are the ones who discover that they have been given in marriage to each other as part of the healing process that all people need.

THE BLAME GAME

False perceptions of marriage perpetuated by a culture fixated on paradise are not the only problems. Satan is the destroyer, and his desire is for us to be his partner in wrecking other human beings. One of the devil's favorite strategies is to build up a mirage of false expectations about married life so that we will be disappointed when reality hits home. Satan's hope is that when disappointment sets in, we will lash out at the perceived source of that heartbreak: the person we married.

God is just the opposite. Jesus, the healer and redeemer, wants us to be His partner in mending our mate. Ephesians 5:26-31 makes it clear that the husband is to be to his wife what Christ is to the Church: "So husbands ought to love their own wives as their own bodes; he who loves his wife loves himself. For no one ever hated his own flesh, but nourishes and cherishes it, just as the Lord does the church" (vv. 28-29). A husband is to be a priest of the Word on his wife's behalf and an agent for healing, for "God sent His Word to heal them and to deliver them from all of their destructions" (Ps. 107:20).

When a husband takes on this role—when he sacrificially lays his life down for his wife, just as Jesus laid down His life for the Church—he causes healing to happen in her. The wife has the same role when it comes to her husband. When she is an honoring helpmate the way that God designed (not blindly submitted nor overbearing, but honoring in a godly way), her love heals whatever is wrong with him. There are no exceptions.

HELP! I MARRIED THE DEVIL!

Let me tell you how this truth hit me in my own marriage. First of all, understand that like everyone else, I tried my best to select someone who was just right for me. When I met Karen, I was attracted to her and thought that we were compatible. We got along much of the time and she laughed at my jokes—I really loved her. Of course, while we were dating, I discovered that Karen had issues! I tried to fix everything I could— and in my mind, there was *a lot* to fix!

After Karen and I married, we spent a few great days in Newlywed Bliss. But the day came when we moved out of that special place and I discovered that my wife was more broken than I had originally thought. One day I looked over at her in our bed at Paradise Hospital and thought, *You're so sick! Get up! Get up! Get out of that bed! I need you to come over here and wait on me. I'm hurting!* The first three years of our marriage were just like that. I was bitter. I thought, *I can't believe I married a sick person who can't wait on me.* Despite all my efforts to select and mold the "perfect" wife, the worst possible thing had happened: I began to believe that I had accidentally married *a devil!*

Of course, my wife thought the same thing about me—*and with good reason.* When I married Karen, I was carrying around deep wounds and scars from devastating experiences that I had been through earlier in my life. I was terrified of all that lay hidden inside of me, and I was afraid of my baggage being discovered or opened. As a defense, I developed the personality of a fighter. I masked my deep emotional hurts and problems. Of course, I had issues, too, but I worked hard to keep them concealed.

As a result, when I married Karen, I was basically incapable of being vulnerable or transparent with her. I was afraid of my own emotions, and the more fearful I grew, the more combative I became. In the first three years of our marriage, I verbally beat Karen down, destroyed her with my words, and rejected her—and she did the same to me. We continued on that downward cycle of hurt and rejection until we finally woke up one morning and realized that what we were doing was not right. We couldn't live that way.

As I previously described, God met us in that moment and saved us by His grace. I know I would be divorced eight-times over if it were not for Jesus. He helped us to stop being each other's enemy and to instead begin to be each other's redeemer. That's why I say without hesitation that Karen healed me. She accepted the mess I had made of myself and became God's instrument in helping me deal with feelings, facts, problems and hang-ups.

By God's grace and through His power, I've done the same for Karen. After three years of beating her down, I have spent the last 30-plus years building her up. I have had the privilege of being God's instrument in her healing.

Karen and I went through hell together and came out on the other side. As a result, today, we are deeply in love and have a fantastic marriage. We decided that whatever we went through, we were going through it together, as partners.

That's our story. It worked for Karen and me, but does the healing journey work for others? Yes! I can tell you dozens upon dozens of stories, but I will limit myself to one that ably shows how it all works.

Karen and I have a friend who entered into marriage believing that her groom was the confident football hero she knew in high school. What she didn't know was that beneath his easy-going façade, he hid a horrible anger problem. One Saturday morning shortly after they left Newlywed Bliss, she watched from her living room as he threw a lawnmower against a tree because it wouldn't start. Our friend immediately phoned her mom and yelled, "I married a crazy man, Mother! Get me out of here!"

Our culture promotes the concept of marrying the perfect bride or groom. Romance novels and chick flicks promote an unrealistic image of well-groomed, domesticated men who enjoy nothing but shopping for antiques and sharing their feelings all day long. Of course, that's not the way it is. Men are frequently a lot more disgusting than that!

Once a woman marries, she usually watches the "perfect" man morph into something altogether different. When the real man starts to emerge, the temptation for the woman is to grow cynical, sarcastic and bitter. Her gut reaction is to back away and reject him when he needs her the most. (Of course, this can also happen for the husband when he sees his new bride throw a lawnmower against a tree!)

The devil's strategy is to implant in a person's mind this unrealistic view of what a mate should be so that we will reject our husband or wife when he or she doesn't live up to expectations. (Remember, the devil's plan is to get us to be his co-destroyer of another human life. The Lord's plan is to get us to be a co-redeemer of another human life. And we can't redeem another person until we are willing to accept who we really are.)

Think about it. As Christians, our problems didn't all go away the day we met Jesus. But the day that we met Jesus, we met a healer who was committed to a life-long process of restoration. Likewise, our emotional and relational problems didn't disappear the day we got married. But the day we got married, we met the agent of our healing. We're each other's patients, and we're each other's doctors. Karen is my patient and my doctor, and I am hers. That means going to hell together and coming out the other side.

The way we build a lifetime of love—and a great marriage—is by getting into the trenches and solving every problem that comes our way. We must fight the enemy together.

You may say, "Well, I don't want to go through hell in marriage." Well, you can wish all you want, but that will not change reality. Get ready. Though some people are more damaged than others, once married, everyone goes through some "worse," some "sicker" and some "poorer" times.

As I've already noted, the fundamental reason for divorce isn't money, sex or communication. It's disappointment. It's "I wanted something better—but I got you." Like C. S. Lewis's Wormwood, the devil sits there whispering, "That's exactly right. You picked door number 1 when you should have picked door number 2! The person behind door number 2 would have been so much better. They wouldn't have all these problems and hang ups."

The scenario is all too typical. At the very moment that we ponder the devil's lie about door number 2, we see an attractive girl in line at Starbucks, on the elevator at the office, or on the pages of some magazine. If we really let our imagination run wild, we recall old yearbook photos and the list of girl's we once wanted to date—should have dated! Let me tell you, everybody looks good from a distance. But when you get up close, we are all the same: damaged goods.

FIRST STEPS TO HEALING

Regardless of how hard we try to find "the one" and no matter how much effort we put into making the courtship, wedding and honeymoon just right, we are all going to wake up one day and see some things in our mate that we never expected to find—needs and deficiencies that can be shocking. When that stunning revelation comes, our natural tendency will be to stay perpetually alarmed over the deficiencies of our spouse and, at the same time, totally preoccupied with our own hurts. But this is not the way to get released from Paradise Hospital.

In fact, the way into health and paradise is to do the opposite of our natural tendencies. We must get up, raise our spouse out of bed, and tend to him or her. We must help each other to the door and take a walk outside. Once we do, we'll discover that paradise is right outside.

We don't have to wait! We can begin the healing process the first day we get married. All we have to do is refuse to accuse and attack each other from the outset. Instead, we need to look at our spouse's problems and say, "You know something, I see that you're damaged, but God has given me the privilege of loving you into health and wholeness! God has given me the ability to fix your hurts through my words and my love." Each day that we choose to help each other in this way, our walks in paradise will become longer. Gradually, we will leave the hospital farther behind, until one day it becomes nothing but a distant memory.

At least half of the people who check into Paradise Hospital die there—their marriage ends in divorce. Others stay in the hospital and never step out—they exist in joyless and unhappy marriages and remain bitter for the rest of their lives. Of course, either scenario could have been prevented if the couples had just understood the real challenges that they would need to overcome together and the blessings that could have been ahead for them.

Thus, there are two basic realities about marriage that we must confront if we are to enter our secret paradise. First, we all have hurts from our past, quirks in our personalities, and ignorance concerning the opposite sex. We're all ailing and damaged. There are no exceptions. Second, when we enter into it properly, marriage is a healing journey. We are designed by God to heal each other.

I know, nobody ever told us that paradise begins in the ICU ward! But the sooner we accept this fact, the sooner we can move on to life after the honeymoon and develop a happy and successful marriage.

Note

1. Barbara Dafoe Whitehead and David Popenoe, *National Marriage Project, 1999, 2002. Rutgers University.* http://marriage.rutgers.edu (accessed February 14, 2006).

CHAPTER 3

Reality Weddings!

As we've seen, a beautiful storybook wedding ceremony is poor preparation for waking up in Paradise Hospital. And given that every couple will have to survive this shock of reality in order to move on to the paradise of helping and healing one another, I would like to make a proposal that is based on some of the reality-based TV programs that fill the airwaves these days. I think we should start having reality weddings.

Here is how it would work. First, just as every contestant on a reality TV show is carefully screened, every couple who wants to get married would be required to go through intense marriage counseling. The purpose of this counseling wouldn't be to "fix" the couple, but to diagnose each person's true emotional condition. The session would be documented in a report from the psychologist and forwarded to the officiating pastor. The couple would then be dressed for their wedding according to what the psychologist judges to be each person's true emotional condition.

REALITY CEREMONIES

Remember, this is a *reality* wedding, so the groom will not be sharply dressed in a dapper tuxedo. No, that would be false advertising based on what is now known about his true emotional condition. Instead, we will dress our groom in a military uniform, because his home was a war zone growing up. Since he is emotionally wounded and battered, we would puncture his uniform with bullet holes and tear his sleeves.

We would pour blood all over him, bandage his head, and break his leg. All of this would give us a more accurate representation of the condition that our groom is really in.

Now, we can't leave out his family—after all, they're also part of the wedding party—so let's also dress them in camouflage fatigues and leave them shot up, bloodied and bandaged on the front pew. Keep in mind, all of this is just to help give the bride an accurate picture of the *reality* of her situation. These are things she needs to know right up front.

Of course, the groom also needs an accurate picture of the condition of his bride. So, instead of dressing her up to look like a fairy-tale princess, we'll put her in a hospital gown and give her a pair of crutches to help her limp down the aisle.

The bride's family is also an emotional train wreck, so let's put her father in a hospital gown as well and have him walk her down the aisle while pushing an IV trolley. Then we'll line up the other members of her family, all on life support, on hospital gurneys against the side wall of the church.

This is reality.

The pastor who conducts the ceremony will be dressed as a terrorist and will carry an AK-47 during the entire ceremony. As the couple recites their vows, the minister will hold them at gunpoint and order, "For better or for worse! Say *worse* like you mean it! For richer, for poorer. Say *poorer* again. I CAN'T HEAR YOU!"

All of this will give the bride and groom a much more accurate picture of just what they are committing to. I suspect, however, that this type of ceremony will not catch on. People are probably going to stubbornly cling to their pretty weddings in fancy clothes.

So I have a back-up plan!

REALITY VOWS

My alternative plan involves a new kind of vow—reality vows. If everyone is going to insist on dressing nice, we could at least revise the vows in a way that will better set up the couple for reality.

My reality vows would go something like this:

I do solemnly swear to take you as my life-long patient.
To bandage and to medicate you as long as we both shall live.
I will love you for richer or for poorer, for better or for worse, and in
sickness and more sickness, because you are one sick puppy!
I don't see you getting well anytime soon, but I am hoping for some
modest improvement today.

I realize that the pretty clothes you are wearing right now, on this our
wedding day, are rented and will have to be returned.
You will probably never look this good again.
This is why we are taking so many pictures to preserve this rare
moment.

I also understand that reality is waiting for me at our hotel room, where
tomorrow your powerful morning breath will announce the dawn of
our lifelong journey together, and the harsh morning light will reveal the
real you.

In spite of all of this, I love you with all of my heart and wholly commit
myself to this marriage, until death do us part, so help me God—because
I'll need all the help I can get.

These reality vows probably have no greater chance of acceptance than the reality wedding. But you get my tongue-in-cheek point: Unrealistic expectations of marriage can lead to disappointment and, ultimately, the death of the marriage. Remember Jesus' approach: "If you want to follow Me, let's get something straight: It could cost you everything you have. Be prepared for the worst."

If you enter marriage in fantasy mode and think, *We're okay—any problems or issues we have will be burned away by the intense fire of our love,* you are setting up yourself and your marriage for disappointment and failure. But if you enter marriage knowing that you and your spouse have made a commitment to get through whatever comes your way, there is no way your marriage will die as a result of disappointment. In fact, you'll discover that it is much better than you thought. And every day that you fulfill your responsibility to do what God wants you to do, your marriage will become better and better.

TRIUMPHANT REALISM

Yes, shortly after the honeymoon all newlyweds find themselves in Paradise Hospital, but you don't have to stay there. So quit focusing on your needs, and stop accusing your spouse of failing to meet them. Instead, get out of your bed, limp over to your spouse's bed, help him or her up, and then take a walk in the sunshine of God's grace.

When you do that, you will begin to experience marriage the way that it was designed. You will get better each day, until one day you are healed, whole and living the way that God intended. It's a secret to a lasting marriage. It's called *triumphant realism*. (Its negative counterpart is "naïve optimism," which breeds nothing but disappointment.)

This is not pessimism, mind you. If you live your life with a pessimistic attitude toward marriage, you will not survive, because you won't have the faith that you can succeed. Triumphant realism says, "It's not going to be easy. There are going to be challenges. But we are going to make it because we are committed to the final outcome of doing the right thing and believing God for the results."

When you take the path of triumphant realism, not only will you have discovered the secret to a marriage that survives, but you will also be well on your way to the second secret of paradise in marriage—the secret ingredient that is always present in every really great marriage.

Get real and read on.

SECRET ONE

Triumphant Realism

Realize that you and your spouse
are hurting, flawed people who
need restoration and healing. And
know that while it won't be easy,
with God's help you and your
spouse can be made mutually
whole, happy and fulfilled for life.

A Redemptive Spirit

Damaged people carry a heavy burden of pain from years past. Somewhere deep within there lurks a huge black spot of hurt, anger and despair. It is rarely if ever acknowledged. They have suffered at the hands of others with the issues never having been resolved.

Rev. John Simpson, Victoria, Australia

CHAPTER 4

Radical Redemption

Early in my ministry, a woman came into my office and told me a story that I had heard many times before—and unfortunately would hear many times again: "My husband is having an affair." In this case, the woman's husband was living part-time with her and the family and part-time with the other woman.

"He comes to the house three or four nights a week, eats, and changes his clothes," she said. "He makes it known to me and the kids that he also lives with this other woman. He goes back and forth, and has been doing so for several months. I've said everything I know to say to him—I've even threatened him—and I do not know what to do."

"Well, you obviously have grounds if you want to divorce him," I told her. "Is that why you are here, to seek my counsel regarding a divorce?"

"No," she replied. "I don't want a divorce. I want to make the marriage work if I can."

"Well, I think I can help you," I said. "I'm going to give you a strategy for winning your husband back. First, the next time he comes home, I want you to make his favorite meal, dress up nice, put makeup on—in other words, do everything that you know your husband likes. Whenever he is in the house, I want you to consider what you would do if Jesus visited your house, and then treat your husband the same way."

The more I talked, the more I saw her countenance fall. "Did you hear what I said about my husband?" she said.

"You just told me that you wanted to try to restore the relationship," I reminded her. "If you want to divorce your husband, that's fine. You have the legal right. If that's what you want to do, you need to go talk to an attorney. But you told me that you wanted to redeem your marriage."

"Yes, I do. We've got kids. I do not want a divorce."

So I repeated, "Well, I am telling you how to do it. Go home, and when your husband comes in, I want you to treat him like you would treat Jesus Christ."

"Should I have sex with him?"

"It is your right not to do so because he is having an affair," I said. "It might be that you shouldn't have sex with him again until the affair is broken off. You can if you want to—that's between you, the Lord and your own conscience. However, apart from sex, I want you to talk to him and treat him as you would treat Jesus. Do you understand?"

"Yes, I understand."

"If you do this, it will get his attention," I assured the woman. "And when he asks you why you are doing this, tell him it is because a man at church told you to do it. Then ask him to come and see me."

"Pastor Jimmy, there's no way he's coming to see you. My husband is not saved. He is a very unrighteous man."

"Trust me," I said. "His curiosity will get him in here. And there's one other thing I want you to do. I want you to repent to him."

"What!" she exclaimed.

"When he is in the house, and when you have done all these things, you should repent to him. Tell him everything that you have done wrong."

"You're serious, aren't you?"

"Yes, I'm serious. I don't want you to talk about all the things that he has done wrong. I want you to go up and say to him, 'I have verbally abused you in my anger.' You *have* verbally abused him, haven't you?"

"Well, yes, I have said a lot of bad words."

"Tell him that. Talk about your verbal abuse and your dishonor. Have you treated him as you would treat Jesus before?"

"He acts like the devil. Why would I treat him like Jesus?"

"You should repent to him for not treating him as you would treat Jesus."

The woman's eyes were now glazing over and she was looking at me with a dead stare. There was no mistaking that this was one very troubled sister.

"You don't have to do this," I said. "As I told you before, if you want to divorce him, you have biblical standing to do so. I am just saying this to you because you came into my office and told me that you don't want a divorce. I am giving you a strategy for winning him back. Are you okay?"

"Yes, I think I am okay."

THE RESULTS OF REDEMPTIVE BEHAVIOR

One week after the conversation in my office, the woman came back to update me on the results.

"I've certainly got my husband's attention," she said. "When he came home the first night, I had his favorite meal cooked. He ate it without saying a word to me and then went into the living room. I followed him in and just sat there with him. I had some music on. I did everything that you suggested I do. I waited on him all night. Finally, he dropped the newspaper that he had been holding in front of his face and said, 'What are you doing?'

"So I told him, 'You know something, honey? I've been going to a counselor at church. He has told me that I am wrong.'

" 'Really! He told you that *you* were wrong?'

" 'That's right. I want to repent to you for the bad things that I have said to you, for dishonoring you and not treating you the way I would treat Jesus, and for all the times I became mad and said things that I shouldn't have. I am sorry. I want you to forgive me.'

"He put the newspaper back in front of his face. Then I told him you wanted to see him—that definitely got his attention. Anyway, this week, he came home five nights instead of his typical three or four. He just kept coming around, kind of looking at me. You know, sort of a fly-by."

I listened to her entire report, happy that she had followed through on my advice, but not at all surprised by the positive results.

"Do you think he is going to come see me?" I finally asked.

"He's thinking about it. What do I do this week?" She was ready for more.

"Keep it up, and tell him again that I want to see him."

The next week, her husband came to my office with her. It was the funniest sight. She walked in the room and sat down. Then he walked in, cool, not saying anything. He just looked around the room, and at me. I shook his hand and welcomed him to come in and sit down.

"I heard you two are having some marriage problems," I said.

"Yeah, we got problems," the husband admitted. "Guess you know I'm living with another lady—going back and forth."

"That's what I heard."

"Been doing it for a long time," he added.

"I heard that, too. But as I was talking with your wife, it seemed to me as though she was doing some things that might possibly be contributing to your behavior. I don't believe that what you're doing is right—and I don't believe that she should be blamed for it—but I told her that I thought she could change some things."

"Yeah, she's doing really good," he smiled. "She's doing really good, *really* good."

"How about you, how are you doing?"

"I'm not doing so good."

"That's what I hear," I acknowledged. "You know what I think? I think that God put you two together, and that He's got a purpose for your marriage. And I think the devil's trying to destroy that purpose. I also think that God brought you to my office today so that you could give your heart to Him. What do you think?"

The man didn't miss a beat. "I think you're right," he said.

That day he received Christ and not only became a strong man of God, but also one of my favorite people on Earth. It was absolutely awesome.

LOVING AS CHRIST LOVED

Six months later, the husband was the one in my office.

"I need to talk with you about my wife," he said. "She's got some problems."

The man had a long list of things his wife was doing that he considered wrong. She was very intelligent, articulate and capable of being abusive with her words. This man was now becoming the leader in their home and an awesome husband and father, but his wife did not realize how the habits that she had developed from her past hurts were undermining him and the growth of their relationship.

"Remember the little conversation I had with your wife?" I said to him. "Well, now it is your turn. Please, go home and love her in the same way that Jesus loves the Church."

The husband needed to redeem his wife just as his wife had done for him. The man went home, changed his behavior and started loving his wife as Christ loves the church. As a result, this couple grew and became an even more godly family.

A SHOT IN THE DARK?

Maybe you are thinking, *Pastor, I see that your counsel worked for that marriage. But wasn't it kind of a shot in the dark? That relationship was extreme!*

No, it wasn't a shot in the dark. It was the application of a biblical principle of loving as Christ loves the Church and showing respect that is at the core of every relationship. When this happens, radical redemption is possible.

IMPORTANT NOTE

Jesus, of course, is the only true Redeemer. We can never replace or duplicate His work on the cross (the original Redemption). All redemption comes from Christ, and when we allow His life, power and values to transform us, we become redemptive people. Not only are we redeemed individually, but also the work of redeeming can go on through us. We can help bring a measure of redemption to others. In marriage, the man is to love his wife as Jesus loves the Church (see Eph. 5:25). And the woman is to respect the man. These are solid redemptive models. Christ works through us by the power of the Holy Spirit, and in this way we too become redeemers.

CHAPTER 5

Acts of Redemption

Restoration in a marriage starts with an act of redemption. For the man and woman whose story I told in the previous chapter, the wife, who was being unjustly treated, took the first step. She had come into my office with grounds to divorce her husband. Quickly, she discovered that she had contributed to the couple's problems—that she had attacked her husband with words, which had driven him farther and farther away.

Clearly, the husband's affair was not her fault. Yet she chose to step forward and introduce into their relationship a secret element that is a key to every great marriage. She brought to their husband-wife relationship *a redemptive spirit.*

When a couple invites redemption into their marriage—regardless of where they have been or where they are now—their relationship will not only last through troubled times but it also has a great chance of becoming fabulous.

Of course, this principle can be found in the Bible. In 1 Peter 2:18–3:7, the apostle Peter tells us why redemption is essential. Alhough this is a long passage, please read it all as it truly sets the stage for paradise in marriage.

> Servants, be submissive to your masters with all fear, not only to the good and gentle, but also to the harsh. For this is commendable, if because of conscience toward God one endures grief, suffering wrongfully. For what credit is it if, when you are beaten for your faults, you take it patiently? But when you do good and

suffer, if you take it patiently, this is commendable before God.

For to this you were called, because Christ also suffered for us, leaving us an example, that you should follow His steps: "Who committed no sin, nor was deceit found in His mouth"; who, when He was reviled, did not revile in return; when He suffered, He did not threaten, but committed Himself to Him who judges righteously; who Himself bore our sins in His own body on the tree, that we, having died to sins, might live for righteousness—by whose stripes you were healed. For you were like sheep going astray, but have now returned to the Shepherd and Overseer of your souls.

Wives, likewise, be submissive to your own husbands, that even if some do not obey the word, they, without a word, may be won by the conduct of their wives, when they observe your chaste conduct accompanied by fear.

Do not let your adornment be merely outward—arranging the hair, wearing gold, or putting on fine apparel—rather let it be the hidden person of the heart, with the incorruptible beauty of a gentle and quiet spirit, which is very precious in the sight of God. For in this manner, in former times, the holy women who trusted in God also adorned themselves, being submissive to their own husbands, as Sarah obeyed Abraham, calling him lord, whose daughters you are if you do good and are not afraid with any terror.

Husbands, likewise, dwell with them with understanding, giving honor to the wife, as to the weaker vessel, and as being heirs together of the grace of life, that your prayers may not be hindered.

The standard Peter sets forth here is not simply for servants and their masters, but it also works in all relationships—specifically in marriages. He was declaring that believers are called to be redeemers, similar to the way Jesus was called to be and remains our ultimate Redeemer.

ACTS OF REDEMPTION

The word "redemption" means to pay a price for someone else. A redemptive act mends a person, bringing him or her back to where he or she ought to be—back to his or her created order of being. Redemption further implies that the person needing repair cannot restore himself or herself—someone else must do it for him or her.

When humankind rebelled against God, we could not redeem ourselves. The gap was so wide that God had to provide the ultimate act of redemption on the Cross and through the Resurrection. When it comes to our need for personal salvation, no one but Jesus can be our Redeemer. We cannot bring ourselves back to a right place with God, and neither can a spouse. We can only return through Jesus, who is the source of all redemption.

While we sometimes get to participate in the process, we should never forget that there could not be any redemption, not even in marriage, if Christ had not shed His blood. With that said, let's look further at how God allows us to participate in acts of redemption in marriage.

In the passage above, Peter was writing to believers in extreme situations. Think about it: In a culture and age in which it was possible for one person to be owned by another, the first example that Peter gave of being a redeemer was not how a master could minister to his servant, but how the servant should relate to his master. And notice that his example was not about what the servant should do when he or she was being treated well, but what the servant should do if he or she was being mistreated (or treated unjustly): "When you are being mistreated by someone, do not return evil with evil" (1 Pet. 3:9).

Of course, Peter made it clear that the opportunity to be a redeemer does not exist for the person who is being punished for doing wrong (or justly): "For what credit is it if, when you are beaten for your faults, you take it patiently?" (1 Pet. 19-20). Only the person who is being treated unjustly can turn around and honor the person who is abusing him or her. Only in response to baseless chastisement is there the opportunity and need for a redemptive spirit.

Why would we choose to offer redemption to those who have treated us unjustly? Peter explains: "For to this you were called, because Christ also suffered for us" (1 Pet. 2:21). We offer redemption to others because this is what Jesus did for us. Because of our sins, we have all treated Christ unjustly, yet Jesus took our sins in His body and redeemed us through the

Cross. Now, He calls us to do acts of redemption for others.

Christ exemplified how to respond when we are mistreated for doing good. When He was sinned against, He did not sin; when He was reviled, He did not revile in return. Instead, He kept entrusting Himself to God, the Father, who judges righteously. And because of that choice He made, though we were messed up, we are now able to come back. Through Christ's righteous behavior, He has redeemed us. As a result, we are called to go and—through our righteous behavior—help bring redemption to other people who are doing wrong.

That's a fuller picture of redemption. It is essentially an act of doing something right to others who are doing us wrong in order to win their heart and the relationship. It means not fighting a wrong spirit with another wrong spirit, for the only way we can defeat a spirit is with the opposite spirit.

Only love can defeat hate. Only mercy can defeat judgment. Only grace can defeat maltreatment. Jesus fought evil with good. If we ever expect to see redemption, we can do no less.

THE PERFECT WIFE (OR HUSBAND)

First Peter 2:18-25 was merely the apostle's introduction to the instruction that followed: In the same way that servants should offer redemption to their masters when they have been treated unjustly, wives and husbands should offer redemption to each other (see 1 Pet. 3:1,7). Why was having a redemptive spirit such an important ingredient in Peter's formula for a successful marriage? Because every believer carries the knowledge that he or she is whole and saved because of a redemptive spirit.

Some people believe that the way to avoid issues in marriage is to find a potential mate who has no issues, no hurts and no problems. Sorry to burst any bubble that you might have, but such a mate doesn't exist. There is no such thing as a whole, healthy husband who has not been the focus of some redemptive activity by his wife. Every husband has to be redeemed. Every whole, healthy wife is one who has been redeemed by a good husband. If we are not willing to engage in redemptive behavior within our marriage, our marriage will never work.

Years ago, I conducted a ceremony for a couple. Each came from a good Christian home, had a good upbringing and were attractive, well-educated and sharp. If ever there were a perfect couple, it would have been these two people. When this couple came in for counseling, I discovered that they had spent a great deal of time preparing for their marriage. This couple did everything. I was very impressed with their diligence.

Everything seemed perfect. But as the young man began telling me about how he viewed their marriage, I became troubled. "For the past 12 days, I have sent her a white rose—white representing purity, and 12 representing the number of government," he told me. "I want the government of our home to be based upon purity. Today, I sent her seven red roses because red is the color of sanctification. I want our marriage to be sanctified before God."

The young man was over the top, and he went on and on like this. As he spoke, I noticed that his fiancée was smiling, kind of looking at him. He was a very handsome guy, well-educated, and seemingly perfect in every way. But he was just *too* good. I thought, *Honey, if you think you are getting by without redeeming this guy, you're wrong. You're going to have to help redeem him.*

Most often, this process of redemption in marriage begins with the wife. When the apostle Peter wrote, "Wives, likewise, be submissive to your own husbands," he was not picking on them. He was acknowledging the fact that women are naturally more relational than men and often the first to recognize the need for redemption in the relationship. In fact, 95 percent of all marriage counseling is initiated by the woman.[1]

What I have seen almost without exception is that after the wife acts to redeem her husband, she falls apart and her husband has to act to redeem her. By "falling apart," I mean that she finally finds herself in a place where she can display her own vulnerabilities and weaknesses—things she could not show or deal with before because she always had to be strong for her husband. This was the case in the story of the couple in the previous chapter: Once the husband became a loving husband and father, the wife had to deal with the habits that she had developed because they were now damaging their relationship.

Separation or Healing

What each of us must realize is that a redemptive spirit is not required because the relationship is bad or wrong. It is required because all meaningful relationships hurt. There is no such thing as a meaningful, close relationship that isn't going to hurt. If we want to have close friends, it is going to hurt. As much as we desire otherwise, if we are going to be married and have an intimate relationship, we have to acknowledge and deal properly with the pain that we cause each other.

That's impossible to do without a redeemer in the relationship. Both spouses will do the wrong thing with those hurts, and those words and actions will ruin the relationship. Our sins—especially the sins we commit with our mouths—will hurt each other.

Not only do our sins hurt each other, but also our immaturities hurt us. I once attended a birthday party that an acquaintance threw for his wife. As I walked up to him, I heard him whispering to his buddies about the present he had bought his wife. "Look what I got my wife for her birthday . . . a fishing boat!" he said. He had bought her a $30,000 fishing boat!

"I didn't know she fished," I said.

"She doesn't," he responded.

You're dead, I thought to myself. *You'll be buried in that fishing boat, pal. They will find your body underneath. You'll pay for being that dumb!*

Of course, it's not only our immaturities and sins that hurt each other. We also create pain by our insensitivity.

I have a friend who is one of the nicest people you would ever want to meet. But he is also one of the most insensitive. One night, after about 10 years of marriage, he was lying in bed next to his wife with the lights off and reminiscing about how great his life was. After a few moments of silence, he turned to his wife and told her, "You know something? I have never been this happy in my entire life. It just seems like everything is going right."

In the darkness, he heard his wife sobbing.

"What's wrong with you?" he asked.

"I have never been so miserable in my entire life," she replied.

"What are you talking about?"

"You have been totally insensitive to me. I sure am glad that you are happy, because I am miserable."

The problem was that none of her needs were being met. It was just one more instance of how—whether by our sins, our words, our immaturity or our insensitivity—we are going to hurt each other in any important relationship. The question that each of us must answer is whether we will do what the apostle Peter said that we were called to do in those situations. We can either respond to those hurts in a way that will bring separation or in a way that will bring healing to our marriage.

Note

1. Barbara Curtis, "The Truth About Boys (and Girls)," *Christian Parenting Today,* January/February 2001. http://www.christianitytoday.com/cpt/2001/001/1.26.html (accessed February 2006).

CHAPTER 6

From Pain to Paradise

When we think of paradise, we envision a tropical isle or a Rocky Mountain vista. In the introduction to this book, we saw ourselves as already being there, swaying on a hammock or picking Aspen daisies. What we didn't see was what it took to create the paradise and all of the obstacles that we would have to overcome in order to get there.

The truth is that paradise doesn't just happen like some magical moment in a Hollywood movie. The stage must be set, and that takes work. Before we can take a stroll on an atoll in the South Pacific, we must earn enough money to make the trip. We have to make arrangements, buy tickets, take our shoes off for security at the airport, exchange money into some unfamiliar currency, interact with a taxi driver who doesn't speak our language, and put on swimming trunks that no longer fit—and that's the easy stuff. If our luggage is lost, our flight is canceled, we get in a fight with our spouse, or we contract some strange sickness along the way, getting to paradise can be a downright pain. And that is only one piece of the paradise process. Think about the plate movements, volcanic eruptions and galaxy-spinning climate swings that molded and shaped the island, ocean and sun that make up our slice of paradise.

Adam and Eve are the only ones who were born in paradise. The rest of us have to work to get there, and usually that means suffering pain along the way.

WHEN PAIN STRIKES

Pain will come, of that we can be sure. How we react when something goes awry affects much more than just the moment or issue at hand. By pain, I mean any of the myriad pitfalls, disasters or disappointments that strike after we move out of the Newlywed-Bliss Room and into Paradise Hospital. Our reaction to pain can actually determine how long it takes to get to paradise, or it can keep us from ever getting there. So this means that it is important to understand how we respond to pain and how to counter it. When we get hurt, we'll typically react in one of five ways.

1. Repression

We often cope by hiding how we really feel. We tend to stuff whatever hurts deep inside. When we bury our anger, we never reach the point at which we can resolve the original issue. A gopher may be underground and out of sight, but he can do a lot of damage to a garden. Sometimes when frustrated, annoyed or disheartened we can become passive-aggressive toward our spouse. When this happens, rather than being a conduit of healing, a spouse actually can deepen the wounds.

Many people who come to me for counseling spent decades building up bitterness, yet they cannot explain why they feel such fury. They have buried their wounds so deep that they do not know what caused the original sting and they have no clue as to how to unearth all that has gone awry. The devil, of course, makes things all the worse, contorting, twisting and warping the facts, memories and emotions. No wonder dealing with pain is a pain.

Repressing feelings of hurt is the easiest way to respond, but it is also the wrong way.

2. Rejection

Spouses reject spouses. It happens often, and in many ways. One spouse (doesn't matter whether it is the husband or the wife) can simply say the wrong thing or act in a particularly selfish way (you pick the incident—I am sure that you have a list. Everyone does). The other spouse feels rejected. Insults fly, tears run and emotions erupt. The one who has been stung usually responds either by denying that he or she has been bitten or he or she stings back. Both are acts of rejection.

In the first scenario, the spouse who is the object of the insult (or whatever it was that caused the pain) rejects it out of hand and can actually pretend that it was never said (which, in fact, goes back to point 1 about burying wounds). The other, more aggressive, way of rejection looks like a mirror. It is a case of tit-for-tat. If a wife withdraws from her husband, he responds by withdrawing from her. If a husband says his wife is ugly, she says that he is ugly. If a wife complains that the husband spends too much time watching football, he gripes that she spends too much time shopping.

For many husbands, the rejection response takes a form something like this: The husband comes home from work and his wife is so busy with the kids that she pays no attention to him. So the husband vows to get her back—he'll just sit in front of the television watching ESPN until his wife's eyes roll back in her head. *If she won't do this for me,* he thinks to himself, *then this is what I am going to do to her.* The husband in this scenario was basically saying, "You rejected me so now I am going to reject you!"

Returning rejection for rejection never leads to wholeness or restoration in a marriage. The rejection approach is a terrorizing response in which a person basically says, "I'm going to teach you a lesson—I'm going to teach you not to do this to me."

I have seen many forms of the rejection syndrome in action. None of them work. If we want to get to paradise we need to reject rejection.

3. Revenge

Revenge—which is a common response to pain—can look a bit like rejection, but it is more vicious, and usually involves one-upmanship. I have seen it in countless counseling situations. Typically, the spouse who chooses revenge takes this position: If the spouse's mate does something to hurt him or her, that person does something a lot worse in return. It is like a boomerang. The victim vows to create a spirit of dominance in the relationship in order to train his or her spouse not to mess with him or her. It goes beyond rejection or responding in the same spirit in which the spouse acted. It quickly becomes absolute abuse and domination.

In examining this response, it is important to clarify an important biblical principal regarding suffering and abuse. The Bible makes it clear that we should *suffer* for each other, but this does not mean that we should be *abused* by each other. The suffering we should incur involves giving up of personal agendas, preferring the other person by choice over ourselves and if need be actually laying down our lives for another. All of the right kind of suffering, however, is voluntary. It creates a closer bond and improves that relationship. On the other hand, abuse causes damage. Abuse can be physical or emotional. Abuse that harms can take the form of actually punching a person or it can be an imposed fear that if one person doesn't respond a particular way the other will blow up.

God does not give people grace for abuse that harms another. Instead, He gives them the wisdom to get out from under the abuse and to try to redeem their spouses from a safe location in which they are not directly in the path of injurious words and actions.

4. Righteousness

Some people respond to pain in an honest, loving and timely manner. This is certainly a preferred reaction. It's tremendous when someone has the courage to tell his or her spouse, "You know, honey? I feel like you have been insensitive to me. It really bothered me that you bought me a fishing boat for my birthday. I need to talk about it." It's a good idea when painful situations arise for a husband and wife to just sit down and talk.

This is the best approach, but undoubtedly there will be times when the husband and wife don't agree. What happens then? What happens when he or she doesn't change, even though they have agreed? The husband may say, "Yeah, I know. I shouldn't have bought that fishing boat for your birthday," and then immediately take the boat out on the lake. Or the wife may just sit there looking at her husband and say, "I think you're wrong. I think you're selfish. And I don't agree."

The righteous response can bring agreement and change in the relationship. But it can also lead to honest disagreement in which both parties feel that they are right or are not willing to change behavior. If handled right, this can do some good when responding to pain, but it must be approached with caution lest an honest disagreement becomes divisive.

5. Redemption

Finally, couples can choose to help redeem each other through righteous, proactive behavior. For the seven-hundred and fifty-third time, I shout,

Redemption works! (If you only remember one line in this entire book, remember that one.)

WHY REDEEM?

Why do we need to be redemptive in our marriages? Peter gives us insight:

1. We Owe a Debt of Gratitude to Jesus

First Peter 2:21 reads, "For to this you were called, because Christ also suffered for us, leaving us an example, that you should follow His steps." We owe a debt of gratitude to Christ because He redeemed us from our sin through His redemptive behavior. We are called to likewise offer redemption to others. (See "Important Note" at the end of chapter 4 for more detail about the nature of redemption.)

To see how easy it is to overlook this calling to redemptive behavior, look at a familiar verse from Luke 6:38:

> Give, and it will be given to you: good measure, pressed down, shaken together, and running over will be put into your bosom. For with the same measure that you use, it will be measured back to you.

Jesus said this in the context of redemptive behavior. His instruction was part of His teaching about blessing those who curse us, praying for those who spitefully use us, being gracious to people who are ungracious to us, and being kind to evil people the way that God is kind (see vv. 27-37). That's why Jesus said, "With the same measure that you use, it will be measured back to you." Many people apply this just to money, but the meaning is far greater than that. In the context of what Jesus had already said, He was telling people that God would not give them more grace than they gave away. Another way of looking at this is that God will only give us the same measure of grace that we give to others.

Prior to this, Jesus had said, "Judge not, and you shall not be judged. Condemn not, and you shall not be condemned. Forgive, and you will be forgiven" (v. 37). Do you want mercy? Do you want grace? Do you want someone to redeem you when you are unrighteous? Then give redemption to others when you are wronged instead of seeking out revenge against them. Remember what Jesus said: "You'll get back whatever you give."

2. Redemptive Behavior Characterizes Disciples of Jesus

For a number of years, little bracelets that bear the acronym WWJD (What Would Jesus Do?) have been popular. Peter answered this question when he declared that Jesus would never reject or take revenge but would always redeem (see 1 Pet. 2:21). He would never respond to a wounded person with a hurt and angry spirit; rather, He would redeem and heal.

The mission statement of the Church is to make disciples everywhere. Discipleship means that we want to be like Jesus. What would Jesus do if He were married to a woman who had a bad mouth or a bad attitude—a woman who came out of a very damaged past and who did not know how to be a wife? He would not treat her the way that she deserved to be treated. He would redeem her. (No, I am not suggesting that Jesus was ever married. He wasn't. But it is always good to ask what Jesus would do if He were in our shoes.) What would Jesus do if there were a man who was sinful, perhaps like the prodigal son? I guarantee that He would redeem the man. What would He do with a person who responded to insults with even harsher insults? He would redeem the person. To be like Christ, we must allow that same redemptive spirit to mark our lives.

3. Redemption Is the Only Response That Creates a Lasting Solution

When two people engage in sin, God is not the one at work in their midst. When a husband sins against his wife, and the wife reacts by sinning against her husband to get him to stop sinning, both people in the relationship are blocking any possible solution. In such a situation, the devil is the one who is truly at work.

What would happen if a husband were able to get his mate to do what he wanted through sin? Or a wife was able to get her husband to join her in her sin? Their marriage would be marked by a spirit of fear, which would be a major problem. Healing cannot come when fear prevails. The Bible drives home the point: "Perfect love casts out fear" (1 John 4:18).

Only the person who wins the heart of his or her spouse through righteousness truly wins that mate. That's the way Jesus wins us.

In my own life, I know that there is no way fear could have kept me serving Jesus for 30 years. I serve Christ because I love Him. He won my heart. The Bible says that when He was sinned against, He didn't sin; when He was reviled, He didn't revile in return or utter threats. Jesus didn't have to treat us that way. He could have stood in heaven and said, "Let Me tell you something. You'd better do the right thing, or I will strike all of you dead." We could all be doing the right thing out of fear. But we're not. We're doing the right thing because Jesus redeemed us.

RULES FOR REDEMPTIVE LOVE

Once we commit to following Christ in being a redeemer, we need to know what redemptive behavior looks like, and set some boundaries. What are the conventions of redemptive love? Looking again at the passage in 1 Peter, let's examine the four primary rules of redemptive love.

Rule #1: Do Not Sin, Even If You Are Sinned Against

In the 20 years that I have been counseling couples about their marriages, I have found that in nearly every case it is both the husband and the wife who are sinning. Each person was at least somewhat at fault and was using the other person's bad behavior as a justification for his or her own. This has been true even in situations in which both the husband and the wife were believers.

Here's a secret about justification that we all too easily forget: One day, nobody will be there to blame. We will not be able to accuse our mother, father, brothers, sisters, husband, wife or children. We will not be able to blame the government, our neighbors, our pastor or anyone else. We will not even be able to blame the mailman! On the Day of Judgment, regardless of what anyone else has done to us, we will have to stand before Christ and be held responsible for our own actions. Another way to look at judgment is that we will be held responsible for how much we were or were not like Jesus.

Jesus is the standard for all our behavior. When we stand before Him on Judgment Day, we will not be able to say, "The reason I am this way is because of my parents" or "Well, the reason I did that is because of my husband (or because of my wife)." Nothing we can say about what anyone else did to us will excuse our behavior. Yet that is what we do all the time. I see it constantly when I counsel married couples.

One of the saddest situations that I had to counsel was between a husband and wife who had been married for 35 years. The couple were really good people and were faithful church members who truly loved God. In fact, they were not only active in church but also effective ministers in that setting. The husband even had a position of leadership in the church.

But they had many problems. The wife had come from the worst background you could possibly imagine—her childhood was a horror movie. She also had a mouth on her. From the beginning of their marriage, she had been very disrespectful toward her husband—very dishonoring and wounding to him.

The husband's response to his wife's wounding and dishonoring remarks was to just go to work. They had lived that way for 35 years, with neither of them taking steps to redeem or fix the relationship. Over time, the husband withdrew from his wife emotionally and physically. Eventually, he had an affair.

Before the affair, no one had any idea of the troubled condition of the couple's marriage. No one knew that they had lived on different sides of the house *for nearly 35 years*.

I became involved when, due to the husband's position of leadership in the church, the affair became a scandal. When I met with him, he immediately began justifying what he had done by telling me about his wife's dishonor and the way that she had treated him.

"I may not have been a good husband to my wife," he said, "but I was a great father to my children."

"Let me give you some information," I responded. "First, you did sin against your wife even though she dishonored you with her mouth—you withdrew from her. And second, concerning your ideas about how great a father you think you are, you cannot sit in your house treating your wife like you did the whole time your kids were being raised and then tell me how good a father you have been.

"Your children needed to see a righteous husband who loved his wife, and they needed to see an example of how to reconcile problems properly. You never showed that to them at any time while they were growing up. Don't try to justify your behavior!

"Your wife is a good woman, and you could have redeemed her years ago if you had done what was right and not sinned."

The husband was trying to justify his sin, wipe it off on her, and then convince me how good a family man he had been in spite of his wife's neglect.

Of course, the man's wife was not acting correctly either. Peter wrote that a woman who wants to be a redemptive wife must have a gentle and quiet spirit, which is precious to God. This does not describe someone who is mousy; it describes a woman who is acting righteously—a woman who does the right thing and trusts God for the right results. (Having a quiet and gentle spirit does not mean that the woman never speaks her mind. Of course, her views are valid—in fact, essential. Moreover, the quiet and gentle approach can be more powerful than a booming and abrasive approach.)

The lesson to be learned here is that when our spouse fails to follow biblical models of behavior, our response cannot be to walk away, check out, go to work as if nothing is wrong, and then try to justify our own bad behavior. The number one rule of redemption is that we've got to do the right thing in the relationship no matter how the other person is behaving.

Rule #2: Never Seek Revenge with Words

At the time of this writing, my twin granddaughters are 15 months old—and they are the most verbal creatures God has ever created! This is anecdotal proof of what we all know. It's no secret that women, in general, are more verbal than men. In fact, a study of children reported that 98 percent of all the noise that little girls make consists of words. On the other hand, only 60 percent of the sounds of little boys are words. Who knows what the other 40 percent are![1]

This natural tendency among women to be verbal may be why the Bible instructs them to guard their speech (this is good advice for men, too). That can be hard when the wife knows exactly how the husband needs to change and wants to make it clear to him. A wise wife, however, will resist the temptation to lash out with words, and instead behave in righteous ways, for this is precious in the sight of God (see 1 Pet. 3:1-2).

The Bible instructs husbands to "dwell with them [wives] with understanding, giving honor to the wife, as to the weaker vessel, and as being heirs together of the grace of life" (1 Pet. 3:7). This does not mean that the husband is superior, but it does mean that the husband needs to carefully consider how he treats his wife. Specifically, as husbands we need to guard how we talk to our wives.

Now men can be talkers, too. All my life, I have never been at a loss for words—often to my own detriment. My mouth gets me in a lot of trouble. I was verbally abusive to Karen—that was my sin. Karen had her own problems, and she was dishonoring to me, but it was no excuse for the damage that I did to her with my words.

In one of our big fights, I attacked her like a prosecuting attorney. I kept coming back at her, beating her down, and just being a total idiot. When she finally walked out of the room, I thought, *Boy, I'll tell you what, I won that one! Game, set, match!* I was feeling good.

But a few minutes later, Karen walked in the room, put lunch on my lap in a little tray, and said, "I love you." Then she turned and walked back out.

Oh, don't do that! I thought. *No, I want to fight!* It was like pouring coals on my head.

This turned out to be a breaking point in our marriage. When Karen acted in a redemptive way, the Lord said to me, "You do not deserve her." In that moment, my heart broke and the idiot inside me started dying.

Karen was redeeming me. She had started praying, "God, change Jimmy." She had started reacting to my unrighteousness with righteousness.

Jesus suffered, but He didn't utter threats. So when our spouse does something to cause us pain, we're not being a redeemer if we threaten divorce, to have an affair or physical abuse. The devil will try to get us to use our mouth to ruin the relationship. We need to stop using our words to try to change our spouse. Except for righteous speech, we must remain quiet—that goes for men and women!

Rule #3: Let God Be the Judge

Sometimes we can become so convinced that we are right that we fail to consider the possibility that we may have judged the situation incorrectly. Instead of trusting God to determine what is right, we take it upon ourselves to remedy the problem and then force our will in the matter. We play both judge and jury—handing out verdicts and then deciding what punishment we will inflict for those perceived wrongs.

Let me give you an example of this. When I became the pastor of a 900-member church virtually overnight, I had no experience at all. I had been in the appliance business with my parents and had never been to seminary or received any formal training in ministry. I had never conducted a church service, performed a wedding ceremony or officiated a funeral—or even paid much attention to that part of the proceeding in the past. In fact, in my first funeral service as pastor, I felt so clueless that I walked up to one of the funeral home directors, introduced myself as the pastor, and said, "I need you to help me out if you would."

"What do you need, son?" he said.

"Well, I've never done one of these before, and I have no idea what I'm doing."

The director paused and glanced at me strangely for a moment. "You're the pastor of *what* church?" he said.

I didn't know anything about anything. The church began to grow in spite of my ignorance and inexperience, but I was terrified. Two of my biggest fears (which went all the way back to my childhood) were the fear of failure and the fear of rejection. I did not want to fail in ministry. So I compensated by working all the time and trying to be all things to all people.

Driven by my fears and my desire to be a successful minister, I began working 12- and 14-hour days. For about a three-year period of time, I focused on the church and turned my heart away from my wife and children. And during that time, I increasingly felt that Karen was not being a good wife to me.

I had an expectation that when I walked in the door, the kids would be perfect and Karen would be standing there like June Cleaver, wearing a smile and an apron. After all, I was doing the work of the ministry! But she was not happy—and she didn't hide it. The look on her face was as if I were feeding her a constant diet of lemon juice. I saw it. I hated it. But I didn't have a clue that I was causing it.

Karen had a reason for not showing any happiness to see me when I came home. I was not meeting her needs. But when I came in at night and saw her just standing there with an emotionless expression on her face, all I could think was, *You know something? You're not a good, godly wife. You have a man of God as your husband, a warrior for the Kingdom! I've been out saving souls and fighting evil all day long, coming home with blood on my sword— and this is what you give me to look at!*"

I was convinced she was wrong, and so one night, I decided to tell her so. "Let me tell you something, Karen," I said. "I resent coming home and you staring me down with all your expectations toward me. I'm working as hard as I can, and I need some support from you."

"You know, Jimmy, I need some support from you, too," Karen said right back at me. "I understand what you are saying, and you do work hard. That was okay for a year or two, but when is it our turn? When do the kids get some of you? Brent needs this, Julie needs this, and I need this, and you've been gone for three years. When do we get you back?"

Her words didn't move me. I drew the line: "You're getting all you can get, and you need to be thankful for it!" To make my point, I decided to start sleeping on the couch. *I am not going to give the sister the benefit of my company*, I reasoned. And I lay on that couch as righteous as I could be. I knew I was right. No doubt in my mind!

For the next three nights, I lay on that couch and prayed, "Lord, change Karen, please change Karen." But on the third night, I heard the Lord say, "Jimmy, you've communicated to your wife that the church is more important than she is. I want you to get up and repent. Walk into the bedroom, repent to her, and stop treating her like this."

"Lord," I said, "I've laid on this couch for three nights to hear this?!" But I knew that it was God speaking to me. That walk into the bedroom that night was the longest one of my life. I knelt next to the bed and said,

"I'm sorry. I can't believe I'm wrong. I can't believe I'm wrong."

In 1 Peter 2:23, we read that Jesus "committed Himself to Him who judges righteously." I had been blindly convinced that I was right. Instead of doing what was right toward my wife and trusting God to be the judge, I had insisted on being the judge. Having judged my wife wrong, I had begun to persecute her when she didn't listen to what I said. Rather than letting God enforce His will, I tried to enforce my will. In the process, all I was doing was deceiving myself and damaging my wife.

It could have ended in divorce. We were on that track if I had not stopped this behavior.

This is the point: Our marriage had as much potential for paradise as any marriage on Earth. All it needed was two people who were willing to be redemptive and healing to one another. A redeemer does the right thing. A redeemer loves and says, "God, I may be wrong in what I have done. I may be wrong in what I believe about my spouse. I'm going to leave the judgment to You. I'm not going to act like the judge and enforcer in this matter. I'm going to do the right thing and forgive and redeem, and I'm going to leave it up to You to decide who's right and who's wrong. If I'm right and if what I'm doing here is right, I trust You to support me in it."

Don't ever lose your confidence that God is on the side of right. Abraham Lincoln said, "Let us have faith that right makes might." If you are doing the right thing, you won't have to enforce it and you won't have to intimidate or verbally abuse others. If you're doing the right thing, God will be your partner to redeem your relationship.

Every marriage hurts. Every marriage is filled with two people who are imperfect. Both you and your spouse are going to make mistakes—that's just the way it is. But if the pain in your marriage accumulates and your only answer is to stuff it until the pain causes you to reject your spouse or to seek revenge, your marriage is going to become a statistic. You're not going to live in paradise.

Only if you choose to be a redeemer—if you decide that you're going to be like Jesus—will you discover the secret to the paradise that your marriage really is. No husband or wife is exempt from this. Each of us must make that choice. And we must continue making that choice. In our marriage, Karen and I no longer get into huge fights or have unresolved disagreements, but on occasion we still irritate each other and do things that the other person doesn't like. We still get to redeem. I still get to choose to do that right thing even when the right thing is not being done to me.

A secret of every great marriage will always be that choice. Will you be a redeemer in your marriage today?

Note

1. Barbara Curtis, "The Truth About Boys (and Girls)," *Christian Parenting Today*, January/February 2001. http://www.christianitytoday.com/cpt/2001/001/1.26.html (accessed February 2006).

SECRET TWO

A Redemptive Spirit

The best marriages have two
redeemers, but the best person
always does the right thing first.
If you're the best person in the
marriage you'll be the first
redeemer in the marriage,
husband or wife.

A Passion That Lasts

What is passion? The more extreme and the more expressed that passion is, the more unbearable does life seem without it. It reminds us that if passion dies or is denied, we are partly dead and that soon, come what may, we will be wholly so.

John Boorman, British artist

CHAPTER 7

More Than Chemistry

We can't talk about success in marriage without talking about *passion*. Every good marriage has passion. By passion, I mean a large supply of positive emotion in the relationship.

Although it's important for a marriage relationship to be characterized by positive emotion—which is an indicator of how well the deepest needs of a marriage are being met—making every action conditional upon what we feel is not a healthy thing to do. Couples will have needs that emotions will not be able to supply. A husband and wife should be committed to doing the right thing regardless of the emotions he or she feels at any given time.

If we can't rely on our emotions to move us to action, on what can we depend? The Bible tells us that every man and woman who has been born again has been given a tremendous resource through faith in Christ. That resource is *God's* kind of love. The Greek language of New Testament times used different words to distinguish different kinds of love. The Greek word for the greatest, highest love—the love Christ demonstrated for us and gave to us—is *agape*. For me to act in *agape* love means that I'm willing to do for you what Jesus would do, regardless of the circumstances or my emotions.

Take note: There are going to be times in every relationship—even in our relationship with Jesus, the most perfect Person in the universe—when we must choose to serve and act purely from our will. There will be times when the emotion to act will just not be there. That doesn't mean that passion isn't there. It means that in the marriage, for the sake of our passion for each other and for our relationship, we will choose to act regardless of what our emotions may or may not be telling us. These acts of love, which come out of the will, become the seeds of a passion that will be more intense and enduring than even the passion of first love.

THE DYNAMIC OF PASSION

Let me tell you how passion was restored in my marriage. Karen and I went to elementary and junior high school together. But with almost 800 students in our Baby Boomer class, we didn't really get to know each other until we were high school sophomores. At age 16, we became best friends. At age 19, we were married. And yes, we had passion in our relationship. But soon after we married, that passion died. We were numb. We fought all the time. I verbally abused Karen and dominated her. She resented it. Before long, we didn't even like each other anymore.

Most marriages do not recover from such circumstances. Thank God, our marriage did. In fact, we recently celebrated our thirtieth wedding anniversary; and the passion is stronger than ever. We're passionate about each other! Karen is my best friend. You already know that it wasn't easy to get to this point, but you may be surprised at how simple it was.

What you are about to discover is that any couple's marriage can be typified by lasting passion. How? Not by luck. Not by faking it. It's something each of us can do. The secret to restoring the passion in marriage has been given to us by Jesus in His words, "Do not lay up for yourselves treasures on earth, where moth and rust destroy and where thieves break in and steal; but lay up for yourselves treasures in heaven, where neither moth nor rust destroys and where thieves do not break in and steal. For where your treasure is, there your heart will be also" (Matt. 6:19-21).

How does a couple store up treasures in heaven?

The only way to eternalize anything is to give it to God. For instance, consider what you do with your time. Any time spent seeking or serving God becomes eternalized time—time for which you are going to reap an eternity of reward. The same is true with money. The money you give to

God is eternalized; it is laid up in heaven. *Whatever* you give to God is laid up in heaven. You're going to meet it again there. But until then, it connects your heart to God while you are still here on Earth.

That's why Jesus said, "Where your treasure is, there your heart will be also." The word translated "treasure" in Matthew 6 is the Greek word *thesauros*.[1] It's where we get our word thesaurus.[2] In English, a thesaurus is a treasure trove of words. The Greek word *thesauros* can mean "a storehouse" or "a treasure chest"—a place where you deposit your treasure. The word translated "heart" in the same passage is the Greek word *kardia*[3] from which we get the word *cardiac* in reference to things of the physical heart. Here, it refers to the center or seat of our passions.

Put those two together, and we can see that Jesus is telling us that wherever we invest ourselves—wherever we put those things that are important to our lives—is where our passion will be, without exception. This is an eternal principle. It cannot be changed. We cannot separate where we are investing ourselves from our passion. The two are always connected.

Look at how this works in our relationship with Jesus. The secret of staying in love with Jesus and having a passionate relationship with Him for the rest of our lives is a prioritized investment in Christ. That's why we give Him the first and best of our money. It's why we give Him the first day of the week (and why we should give Him the first of every day). When we do that on a disciplined, consistent basis, our hearts cannot help but stay with Him.

There's a reason why God tells us to give the first of our money to Him in tithes and offerings. He knows that where we invest ourselves is where our passion will be. Recognizing this, it's easy to see what causes people to lose their passion for Christ; somewhere along the way they stopped laying up their treasures with God in heaven. Consequently, their passion naturally followed their treasure to another place.

Essentially, their passions are "tattling" on them.

If you're passionate about Christ, that fire for Him reveals that you're giving God your best on a consistent basis. He's a priority to you. It's no accident when you're in love with Jesus and passionate about Him after 30 years of following Him. You're doing something to keep that fire stoked. More than likely, that passion is even greater than the emotion-laden love you had for Him at the beginning. Now it is a deep passion that has grown out of purposefully and consistently giving God your best.

Conversely, if you're lukewarm about Jesus, someone (or something) else is getting what only God deserves. Someone else is getting His time; someone else is getting His money; someone else is getting the energies and the talents in you that He should be getting first.

Wherever your treasure is, there will your passion be also.

INVESTMENT, NOT CHEMISTRY

The way that our passions reveal where we've been investing our time and treasure is not that different from the way we first fell in love.

Many people think that "chemistry" is the reason we fall in love with each other. It's true that chemistry may have been the reason we were initially attracted to each other, physically or emotionally. That kind of attraction is often how we match up with someone. But it's not why we fall in love.

When we first meet someone special, there is a natural emotion generated by that first encounter, but that emotion is followed by a process of investing in each other. Initial attraction immediately results in our giving time to the relationship—and not just a little time. We give significant, dedicated time. This new investment begins to show in our talk and in our priorities. Our boss, our friends and other people begin to hear us say in various ways, "Listen, I can't be with you; I'm going to be with this person." That's when everybody starts teasing, "Aw, you fell in love, didn't you?!"

What happened was that we began to invest our time, energy and money in our relationship with one special person. When that person became our place of investment, we fell in love with him (or her). That's the secret of early love. That's the key to why the passion is so strong. We naturally invest a lot at the beginning of the relationship.

The moment I fell in love with Karen—when I saw her and said to myself, *This is the woman I want to marry*—I no longer cared about spending most of my time with friends, many of whom I had grown up with. I no longer cared about those friends in the same way. I had fallen in love with Karen, and I began to give her the time I had been giving to my friends. We fell passionately in love because we were investing a scarce resource (time) in each other.

That very same principle was working in reverse when Karen and I fell out of love. It's no mystery why our feelings changed. After we married, I gradually returned to giving all my time to work, or golf with friends. Little or no time was invested in Karen anymore. I took her for granted. I came home from work tired and sat around the house, believing that I deserved to be waited on.

I thought that being the husband and income earner gave me the privilege of being taken care of. When Karen demanded something of me, I deeply resented it. I gave no thought to investing in her. I had very little understanding of what the Bible says it takes to be a husband and to build a successful marriage!

FOLLOW HARD, HOLD FAST

In Genesis 2:24, God says, "Therefore shall a man leave his father and his mother, and shall cleave unto his wife: and they shall be one flesh" (*KJV*).

The word "cleave" means "to cling to" and "to stay with." It is also defined as "pursue closely," "follow hard after" and "keep fast."[4] In other words, cleaving requires giving some energy to the relationship. We must work at our marriage if it's going to be a success. We naturally work at a relationship when we first enter into it. But after awhile, there is a natural tendency to start taking each other for granted. That is a part of our human nature that we need to energetically resist.

Taking each other for granted is the very way to fall out of love—with each other and with Jesus. When we first get saved, we come to church, read our Bibles, pray and tell everyone we know about what has happened in our lives. It is fresh in our minds what it was like when we were lost. We remember what bondage felt like. And we are very mindful of how wonderful Jesus is and how rich life is now that we are in a relationship with Him.

But when those memories fade, we begin to take Jesus for granted. We're less appreciative of what He has done for us. Of course, we know we should be investing in our relationship with Him, thanking God every day for salvation and following Him passionately. But we don't. Nor do we see that the reason we are drifting apart is that we're redirecting our passion.

When we take what we once gave to God, or our spouse, and give it somewhere else, we redirect our passion. This is laziness. This generates apathy. This means that we're taking what belongs to the relationship with the one we love and investing it somewhere else out of the mistaken belief that we can stop investing and get the same returns. God's Word calls this process the law of sowing and reaping. It's a simple law, and it operates this way: *What you sow, you are going to reap.*

> Do not be deceived, God is not mocked; for whatever a man sows, that he will also reap (Gal. 6:7).

The encouraging thing about this law is that it's more reliable than feeling powerful chemistry or emotions. This principle works the same for everyone. All we need to do is learn how to apply the law of reaping and sowing in a positive direction on a consistent, disciplined basis to reverse any free-fall into lost passion and destroyed relationships.

Notes

1. W. E. Vine, *Vine's Expository Dictionary of Old and New Testament Words* (Fleming H. Revell, N.J., 1981), s.v. "thesaurus."
2. *Oxford English Dictionary* (Oxford University Press, 2005), s.v. "thesaurus."
3. *Vine's Expository Dictionary of Old and New Testament Words*, s.v. "kardia."
4. *Oxford English Dictionary*, s.v. "cleave."

CHAPTER 8

Up Instead of Down

The scriptural principle we just considered in chapter 7—that whatever a man sows he will also reap—is the key not only to understanding how we lose our passion but, more important, how we can ignite once again a passion that will become even more intense and enduring than we ever dreamed possible.

To put this principle to work in your favor, you need to know that it is made up of two parts that have equal weight. The first part is that you reap *what* you sow. The second is that you reap *where* you sow. You cannot sow at work and reap at home. You cannot sow into your children and reap in your marriage. You cannot sow at home and reap at church. Please don't misunderstand what I'm saying; you need to be doing all those things. You need to be working, going to church and raising your children—all of these areas need the appropriate investment of your time and energy. But what you sow in those areas affects only those areas. In other words, you don't reap from your marriage unless you sow in your marriage.

It's quite possible that you're very much in love with your spouse but you've begun to take him or her for granted. Maybe this attitude has even progressed to the point that passion is gone. You're still dedicated to your marriage, but the relationship has soured (in a similar way that my relationship with Karen had soured at one time).

What do you do when this happens?

To stop the negative downward spiral, it's vital for you to understand the negative progression that develops when you do not invest in your spouse.

First, your spouse's jealousy arises because you're taking what belongs to your spouse and directing it elsewhere. When God's Word says, "For this cause a man shall leave his father and his mother," there's only one way to interpret it: Your marriage is the most important earthly relationship in your life. Marriage doesn't work unless you put it first. Your marriage cannot come second to anything other than Jesus Christ; and putting Jesus first will never harm your marriage. Jesus will always be on the side of your marriage being strong, whole and happy.

When a marriage relationship does not hold first place, a type of jealousy invariably arises in the neglected spouse; this is typified by a strong desire for the time, attention and communication that rightfully belongs to him or her. God actually holds this kind of jealousy for His people. Exodus 34:14 tells us that His name is Jealous. "Jealous" means "intolerant of rivalry." If anything else comes before God in your life, He becomes jealous of whatever that thing is.

Even "good" things that put God in second place provoke Him to jealousy for us. The first day of the week, the first of our treasures, the first of our time, the first of our talents—all belong to God. If we give the first part of these things to Him, the remaining part is blessed and we go on with our lives. And our passions remain with Jesus.

In the same way, a natural jealousy sets itself up within our spouses when we take what belongs to them and invest it elsewhere. One of the most common patterns of inciting this kind of jealousy is when a husband begins to take the passion, the pursuit, the time and the energy he once gave to his wife and directs them toward his job, friends, hobbies and other interests. He turns his heart outside of the home. Even when he is inside the home, he can turn his interests outside of the marriage—toward hobbies or sports on television. That's a man's natural negative tendency.

Just as naturally, a wife can become very resentful of that loss. She resents whatever is taking him away from her and what he's investing in and placing before her. It's not that she minds those things in themselves—as long as they are secondary. She doesn't mind, if they come after her and the children. She does mind otherwise. And as a result, many husbands have watched their wives take the love, care, nurture and attention they once received and direct these toward the kids.

Please understand what I'm saying here. Children are very important, but they are not as important as the marriage. There are a couple of things you must remember to keep this idea in perspective. First, your children will have a much more difficult time having a successful marriage of their own, and all the happiness a successful marriage brings, if they don't see you having one. Second, children are (parents hope!) a temporary assignment.

Our children are both grown and gone. Karen and I are still here.

Honestly, one of the greatest things you can do for your children is to teach them to respect your relationship with Jesus and your relationship with your spouse.

Nevertheless, many men resent the fact that their wives are totally exhausted as a result of the attention they give to the children. I was recently involved as a secondary counselor in a situation in which the mother was completely consumed with the couple's small child and had absolutely no energy left to give to any other interest in life, including her husband. Ironically, the result was that she was not raising that child properly.

In another marriage situation I encountered, the husband worked six-and-a-half days a week, causing his wife to become quite bitter. After talking to them, I told him that his wife was very jealous and resentful of the time he gave his work. Then I counseled him, "Sir, could you go to your employer and say that you have four children and you just don't have enough time at home?"

"I've already done that," he said. "You don't get any sympathy where I work. You work what they tell you to work or you don't work there."

"Have you ever thought about changing careers?" I asked.

He looked at me somewhat surprised. "Are you serious? Do you know how long I've been with this company?"

"Well, I think your other option is changing families," I replied. "I think that if you don't change careers, at some point in the not-too-distant future you will be changing families, because I don't think she's going to stay with you much longer in this situation."

When you give all of yourself, all of your time, to things outside of your marriage relationship—whether involuntarily or by choice—the result is a natural jealousy within your spouse.

You Reap *Where* You Sow

Not only do you reap what you have sown, but you also reap *where* you have sown. This latter aspect of the reaping and sowing principle can produce such devastation in a relationship. When you've been sowing somewhere other than in your home, your emotional gratification will begin to come from that place instead of from within your marriage and family.

Not surprisingly, when I turned almost all of my attention to work and golf shortly after our wedding, those activities soon became the sources from which I derived all my gratification and validation. I had been playing golf since I was 10, so I was very good at the sport. It was gratifying, validating and fun to shoot a great score and spend time with my friends on the course.

It wasn't gratifying to Karen. I remember coming home and finding Karen extremely frustrated with me and saying, "Jimmy, can't you just stay home with me and not go golfing today?" This was before our relationship had totally died and she was still reaching out and trying to rescue the relationship. But I wouldn't listen to her.

I wasn't the least bit interested in playing *less* golf. And when I finished playing, I wanted to come home to a good meal, a clean home, passionate sex and a compliant wife. *That*, I thought, *would be a good wife. Instead, I have a bad wife who nags, and I don't like it.* I wasn't going to give in to Karen, because my emotional gratification came not from our marriage but from all the pats on the back—the validation and prestige that my success as a top salesman and being a skilled golf player earned me. *Where* I was sowing was precisely where I was reaping.

The Demand for Your Heart

The third thing that happens in the downward spiral of misdirected passion is that both Jesus and your spouse ultimately begin to demand your heart back. Your spouse begins to complain, "I resent it that you work all the time. I resent it that you golf on your days off. I resent that you're ministering all the time—pouring yourself into other people—when I get nothing of you. I want you to bring it back."

That demand creates an emotional conflict in you. You want to feel one way, but instead you find yourself thinking: *I like work and I like golf, but I don't like you. I don't have any passion for you. I'm sorry. I know that you want me back, but the problem is that I just don't link time with you with positive emotions anymore. Now my positive emotions are with my friends, with sports and with other interests.*

What I didn't find out until later was that the way you fall back in love is to begin to invest in your spouse again. There's nothing mysterious about it. It's the immutable law of sowing and reaping in action.

Karen and I were out of love. We didn't like each other. I was verbally beating up on her and putting her down. And we were having horrible fights. When she came against me and tried to change me, I rejected her. Later, she began to try to redeem me by coming to me and kissing me on the cheek, praying for me and reaching out in different ways. But she was still complaining to me—and thank God she was. Her honesty in trying to make me understand what I was doing to her ultimately changed our relationship.

It was around this time that I told Karen to get out of the house because she was complaining. "Go pack your bags," I told her. "If you don't appreciate anything I do for you, then pack your bags and get out of here. Go back to your mommy and daddy. I don't care."

She stormed into the bedroom and proceeded to cry her eyes out. And that's the night my life changed. Like the apostle Paul, who suddenly could see what he hadn't seen before, the scales fell from my eyes. Until that night, I had truly thought I was Prince Charming. I thought that I was the best guy in the world, and I couldn't understand why Karen didn't appreciate me.

But that night I realized that Karen was about to leave me. I realized that the way we had been living could not go on. I saw that the fighting was out of hand and that I was wrong. When I went into the bedroom to repent, we were out of love, totally numb. I told her I was sorry and that I was going to put away my golf clubs.

"Really?" she asked.

She stared at me in disbelief. Why? Because in our three years of dating and nearly three years of marriage, this was the first time she had ever heard me say the words, "I'm sorry."

"I'm going to hang them up, Karen," I said. "They are not as important to me as you are, and I'm sorry for what I've done. I don't want you to leave. I want us to work on our marriage."

From that day forward, we began to invest in one another. We began to sow into the relationship. What we reaped was a harvest of passion.

And we fell back in love.

CHAPTER 9

In Love Again

Jesus says that disciplined investing is not only the secret of lasting passion but that it is also the secret of falling back in love: "I hold this against you," Jesus told the church at Ephesus in the book of Revelation. "You have forsaken your first love. Remember the height from which you have fallen! Repent and do the things you did at first. If you do not repent, I will come to you and remove your lampstand from its place" (Rev. 2:4-5, *NIV*).

Jesus will not tolerate a love that is less than first in our hearts. In other words, He demands our passion. First love means a passionate pursuit of Christ and His calling. Do you know what Jesus meant when He warned the Ephesians that if they didn't get their first love back He would remove their lampstand from its place? His hearers knew that the lampstand represented God's divine advertising—His seal of approval. (It shouldn't surprise us to learn that Jesus doesn't want to advertise a group of Christians who are apathetic toward Him. It makes Him look bad.)

It's the same in your marriage—you are a walking advertisement for your spouse. I'm an advertisement for Karen. In those early years of marriage, I was a bad advertisement. But that changed.

The workplace is filled with husbands and wives who talk about how bad their mates are, or they silently shout it through their facial expressions, body language and priorities. No husband wants a spouse who launches an advertising campaign about him like that. And what wife would enjoy being married to a husband who placed an ad in the newspaper telling the world how bad she was? But that's exactly what we do to each other when we refuse to invest our time, energies and focus in ways that will produce an ever-increasing harvest of passion in our marriages.

How do you get the passion back? Jesus, in essence, says, "Remember where you fell from, and repent." "To repent" simply means "to change your mind." Changing your mind is not conditional on an emotional response. Just change your mind and start doing the things you did at first. Don't worry about emotions; they will eventually follow action.

So how do you fall back in love? Start investing once again in your marriage. Don't let your emotions dictate your actions. Remember, it's not possible to separate your treasure from your heart. Your passion and your heart are always connected.

When Karen and I were out of love, she no longer trusted me. When I repented and asked her to forgive me, she was honest about it: "Jimmy, you've devastated me with your mouth, and I don't trust you. I'm willing to stay, but I'm telling you right now, I don't trust you. And it's going to take awhile."

I understood.

"Karen, I don't blame you for the way you feel, because I deserve this. I really do. This has gone on a long time and I know I'm going to have to earn your trust. I want you to stay, and I'll prove to you that I mean business."

I was genuinely changed because my eyes had been opened. What I did that night was put away my golf clubs, and not only for the next week; I stopped for several years. When my buddies asked me about it, I told them, "I've got something more important going on. Sorry, you're going to have to play without me." They teased and criticized me, but I drew the line. "You can say what you want," I told them. "I'm not golfing with you anymore; I'm staying at home."

I began to invest time and energy once again in my relationship with Karen. We began to walk together. We began to sit down and talk—something we had not done in a long time because of the way my verbal abuse had driven out of Karen all hope for meaningful communication.

It didn't take long to see results. In just a few days, signs of life began to return to our marriage. It was like the beginning of spring. You could see sprouts of positive emotion budding more and more each day.

After several weeks, a freshness came back to our relationship, and we liked each other again. We were beginning to have some fun; we were laughing. It had been a long time since we had laughed together.

Several months later, we were back in love—and I mean very much back in love. That was 27 years ago. In every one of those 27 years, our marriage has grown better than the year before. Today we are passionately in love.

How do you fall back in love with Jesus? First, remember the heights from which you have fallen. In other words, remember the way it was when you first got saved. Remember how you pursued Him? How you read your Bible? How you couldn't get enough of Him and His Word?

If your passion for Jesus has grown cold, don't try to manufacture it. Instead, identify what you're doing that is different from what you did at first. Then stop giving your time and attention to that activity or relationship. Just don't do it anymore. Change your mind and say to yourself, *I don't want to invest in something that's going to go up in smoke. I want to invest in eternity. I want to lay up my treasures in heaven. I want to give my first and best to Jesus.* When you make that decision, the emotion will naturally follow.

If you will say the same words about investing in eternity in relation to your marriage, you can walk free of the torture chamber that traps those who are slaves to their emotions. Allowing emotions to replace the *agape* love of Christ in us will always lead to a negative downward spiral. Most people in bondage today got there by following their emotions along a downward path of progressive depression and discouragement. The way up is to follow your will instead of your emotions.

Practice by saying, *I'm going to do this. I'm going to discipline myself to do this.* And then act on what you have told yourself. Discipline will always lead to positive emotions. The more you do the right thing, the better you will feel.

When Cain sinned, God said to him, "If you do well, will not your countenance be lifted up? And if you do not do well, sin is crouching at the door; and its desire is for you, but you must master it" (Gen. 4:7, *NASB*). The happiness and sense of well-being and being accepted takes care of itself if you will focus your will on doing the right thing.

TIPS FOR LASTING PASSION

Let me give four practical tips for building intense and lasting passion in your marriage.

First, focus on your own mistakes and commit yourself to making disciplined changes and investments.

Second, deal with the root issues that caused you to turn your heart away. If you turned your heart away from your wife and toward work, is there a reason? Was it because of something your spouse did once or did consistently that hurt you? Did he say something? Is she frustrating you?

In a previous chapter, we looked at how common it is for a spouse who feels rejected to reject his or her mate in return. If that has happened to you or is about to happen in you, recognize and deal with the root issues of why you are turning away. If you are focusing more on your children, your friends, your career, or something else, what in the relationship caused you to do that? If you can't deal with those root issues by just sitting down and talking, then get help. Commit to speaking to a Christian counselor, and listen to what he or she says.

The third tip is to tell your spouse what you've done wrong. Don't point your finger and put the blame on your mate's shortcomings. Sit down with your spouse and say, "Listen, I haven't been giving you my best. I just realized that I've taken you for granted—I've turned my heart away. I want you to know that I'm back and I'm committed."

Don't place any conditions on what your spouse says back to you. In other words, don't turn back toward your spouse based on him or her reciprocating in kind. Sometimes when people act as though they want forgiveness, they're really baiting the other person—fishing for an apology themselves. (When they don't get the desired response, they become even more offended.)

Regardless of what your spouse does, you do the right thing. The best person does the right thing first, and the redeemer does the right thing even when the other person doesn't. Communicate your commitment regardless of what your spouse does.

Finally, build disciplines into your relationship that keep you investing in it. Build some "first things" together.

Karen and I have built some firsts around money, focused time together as a couple, and praying together. For example, when Karen and I get a paycheck, the first thing we do is write a check to the church. We give the first to God. Likewise, we have date nights—regular times together each week that are set. Right now, because we're empty nesters, Tuesday and Thursday nights are our date nights.

If you're not sure about what I mean by date night, date night is a special night to get dressed up and invest a lot of energy. It's a night to go out somewhere—not just sit around eating chicken and watching a movie on TV. There can be other special outings—one or two nights of camping or going to a nearby town. Spend a couple of days together. Get a babysitter and go somewhere. Your relationship will be energized by time spent exclusively focusing on each other.

You may be surprised to discover that the deepest intimacy in life is not sexual—it's spiritual. Karen and I pray together all the time; we're prayer buddies. When you're praying and worshiping God together, it creates the deepest bond you can imagine. It's so important for couples to spend this kind of time together.

These disciplines we've put in place in our relationship are commitments of our will, not our emotions. They are not something we *intend* to do; they are something we *will* do. They are first things.

Without a doubt, the secret of lasting passion in marriage is disciplined investment. Right now you may be out of love and don't feel the passion you once felt. You're not alone. In my experience of marriage counseling, I can't tell you how common it is for a spouse to say, "I just don't love him/her anymore." But if you will take seriously what you have just read, you will begin to see that how you feel is not the problem. Your lack of feeling love is a result of some choices you've made—choices you can change and ignite once again with that first love.

I have to admit that in some ways I'm kind of an old, crusty marriage counselor. I've learned to say "I've heard it all before." Yet I'm not discouraged by the dire pronouncements and clichés of hopelessness I hear in case after case. When I hear another person say, "I just don't love him/her anymore," what I want to say is, "Well, so what?" So what if you don't love each other! Big deal! I'm here to tell you that your attitude is subject to change. Emotions will follow if you will bring your treasure back into the relationship.

Remember that when you say your love (your passion) is gone, it says something about you. Where are you investing? Where have you been sowing? Is it with your girlfriends? Is it with your children? Is it with your work? Is it with a sport? Where are you harvesting for your gratification and validation?

Don't let your emotions dictate your life. Don't let the devil stand there at the side of your dead emotions and tell you that you made a mistake and need a divorce. Don't run off with someone you met on the Internet in the absurd belief that things will be different. (This is happening every day across America—people getting on the keyboard and lying their faces off.)

No, I want you to know that if you've fallen out of love, just admit that you've made a mistake and commit to doing the things that you know will bring the passion back.

Recall Jesus' simple advice: Remember where you fell from; repent; and do what you did at the beginning. The rest will take care of itself.

Disciplined Investment for Lasting Passion

Stop sowing all your time and
energy into other people and
things and instead sow into your
marriage relationship. When you
choose—by an act of the will—to
invest in your spouse, your emotions will follow. The invariable
result will be renewed passion and
a return to your first love.

Friendship

Friendship, like the immortality of the soul,
is too good to be believed.

Ralph Waldo Emerson (1803–1882)
American essayist, poet, philosopher

Faithfulness, Trust and Appreciation

Friendship is a fundamental need of the human heart. Although they shed little or no light on the question of what a real friend is, even the sitcoms that have dominated TV programming in recent years attest to the fact that the subject of friendship—or, more accurately, our deep hunger for friendship and our pain when it is missing—is an ever-present human need.

But the TV sitcoms, soaps and dramas have also perpetuated the myth that we can be driven solely by our selfish desires and still somehow experience meaningful friendship. In reality, just the opposite is true.

Part of the reason friendship is so hard to find stems from our culture's push to immediately sexualize a relationship between a man and a woman. The physical intimacy that many couples get involved in very early in their dating relationship prevents true friendship from ever developing. Many couples, instead of sitting down to talk or going out just to have fun, jump on the fast track to sex. The result is an emotional stunting of the relationship.

Some couples take it a step further. Not only do they meet and begin sexual intimacy very quickly, but they also choose to live together in a pretend marriage before they are actually married. Many try to justify living together by saying, "Before I get married, I want to know this other person intimately to see if we're compatible." Pretend marriage doesn't work, because it's stolen intimacy.

People who live together before marriage experience more abuse, more infidelity, more break-up, more disappointment—more problems in every category—than people who do not cohabit before marriage.[1] A couple that lives together before getting married is 50 percent *more* likely to divorce after marriage than a couple who did not cohabit.[2] The reason for such a high divorce rate in those situations is lack of commitment to the relationship.

The divine purpose of courtship is to get to know each other's hearts, not each other's bodies. The purpose of courting is not to see how good you are together *in* bed; it is to see how good you are together *out* of bed. Think about it: Even a married couple with an unusually active sex life will spend only a tiny percentage of their total relational time having sex. That's why it's so important to develop a friendship with each other and to find out the other person's character.

In contrast to living together, statistics and scientific studies show that women who are married are the most protected women on Earth. Sure, there are some abusive husbands out there.[3] But on the whole, marriage is a highly protecting environment for women.[4] Other relational environments for adult women are not nearly as sheltering.

That brings up another problem too common in our society—the fact that many couples do not date long enough. I think six months to two years is adequate time for a couple to get to know each other well enough to know if they should marry—especially if their courtship is in the right environment. But significant numbers of couples are getting married just a few weeks or months after they meet! Clearly, not all of those relationships are doomed; but a short courtship, a very troubled courtship, or a sexual courtship prevents deep friendship from developing.

Although premarital sex is certainly a growing reason why friendship fails to develop in marriages, it is not the only cause. In many cases, either through neglect or misdirected focus, couples stop pursuing the goal of becoming best friends. That's certainly the way it was with Karen and me. We began our relationship as friends. Before we married, we spent a lot of quality time together and really enjoyed being with one another. But after we married, the friendship stopped developing and soon deteriorated. We didn't have much fun together anymore. The situation became so serious that we didn't even want to be around one another. So we simply replaced each other with other friends in our lives.

Whatever the reason, marriages that have been robbed of friendship are missing a vital element in making a relationship a paradise. If friendship has grown cold in your marriage or was never given an opportunity to develop in the first place, you can change that. You can turn that lack of friendship around by repenting and taking seven simple steps to becoming best friends with your spouse. The first four steps—*be faithful, believe in one another, embrace your differences* and *be real and transparent* are part of this chapter. The last three steps—*be a place of refuge and safety; be fun, creative and positive* and *bear each other's burdens* will be discussed in the next chapter.

BE FAITHFUL

Recently, I sat on an airplane beside two men who turned out to be a couple of buddies going to a football game together.

"We went on a fishing trip to Canada last year," one of them said, "and I left my wife seven months pregnant and starting early labor pains."

I remember thinking, *I'm going to do a marriage seminar. This conversation will make a great illustration.*

Then he added, "It was okay; she didn't want me to miss the trip."

I was skeptical. "Did you pay a price when you got home?" I asked.

"Oh, yeah, it's all on a voucher system. She got me when I got home. Sure, I guess it affected her. But she'll get over it."

You and I *know* it affected her. And the clear message he sent to her was, "These guys are my friends, and you're not."

The fact is, with every great friend you have, there is always a positive history—a string of sacrifices and choices each of you made for the sake of each other and for your relationship. Without that history, there is no meaningful friendship.

I was preparing to leave for a ministry engagement not long ago whena family member of some close friends was admitted to the hospital with a serious illness. I was busy getting ready to leave, tying up a lot of loose ends. But when I heard the news, Karen and I went to the hospital.

After we stepped outside the hospital room, the father joined us in the hallway and said, "Thank you so much for being there for us, as always. You are true friends."

He was right. That had been true in the history of our relationship. There is always a positive history with friends. The Bible tells us that "a friend loves at all times, and a brother is born for adversity" (Prov. 17:17). Making your wife or your husband your best friend begins with committing yourself to being faithfully there for them, especially when they need you most.

It is within the fire of selflessness and sacrifice that strong bonds of friendship are forged.

BELIEVE IN ONE ANOTHER

No one who consistently criticizes me and puts me down is going to be considered my best friend. I'm just not going to have a best friend who doesn't believe in me. I think you'd say that is true of you too.

James 2:23 says, "Abraham believed God, and it was accounted to him for righteousness, and he was called the friend of God." The reason Abraham was the friend of God was because he didn't question Him. In Genesis 12:1, we read that God told Abraham to leave his hometown of Ur of the Chaldeans. And Abraham left. When God said something to Abraham, he believed it and acted on it. Today, Abraham is the father of our faith.

Our spouses need to hear and see our belief in them. We can't put our spouses down and be negative toward them and think that we can build a strong friendship. Friends believe in one another.

Psalm 100:4 tells us that we enter God's gates with thanksgiving and into His courts—His very presence—with praise. We are built the same way. We receive people into our hearts who come to us with praise and affirmation. Conversely, none of us welcomes a negative person in.

You'll see this truth very quickly in the lives of your children. You will never influence your children until you are able to speak to their hearts. The way to their hearts is by being their greatest friend. You can correct your children all day long and not bring a permanent change in their choices and actions unless they know you care about them—unless they can see that you are their biggest fan.

A story is told of the mother of a little Jewish boy who came home and announced that he'd been expelled from school. Her response was, "I knew it! They don't know how to teach a genius over there." How's that for affirmation?! She was his greatest fan.

This humorous exaggeration illustrates a point. The attitude that causes your children to give you entrance into their lives is when they know that your message to them is "I'm your biggest fan. I am not going to denigrate or disparage you. I am going to believe in you. I am the one who is going to teach you."

When you see the best in your children and you speak the best over them, they open their hearts to you. That's when you have an opportunity to effectively speak into their lives and say, "Don't do that, honey. You're better than that." Your children will tend to rise to your highest expectation.

Likewise, in marriage there are times when we're going to need to be able to speak into each other's lives. We're going to have issues that we need to deal with, corrective things we'll need to say to each other. But to have an entrance to do so effectively requires a foundation of firm belief in one another.

In the old TV sitcom *All in the Family*, Archie Bunker's nickname for his wife, Edith, was Dingbat. Some couples' nicknames for each other are derogatory, and their communication is laced with sarcasm and derision. Perhaps you've heard similar things in your family gatherings. It's one of the most uncomfortable environments you can be in.

Do I need to point out that this is less than conducive to developing friendship? Friendship is inductive—it induces other people toward us. It makes them want to get closer. We naturally gravitate to the place of praise, acceptance and positive belief.

Karen and I work on keeping praise at the forefront of our relationship. I'm Karen's biggest fan, and she is mine. If you were in our home every day, you would observe that the words we speak to each other are overwhelmingly positive. So are the pet names we have for each other.

Why? Because, if you're going to be best friends, you're going to continually do and say things that assure your spouse that you believe in him or her. You're going to do the things that draw you to one another and open you up to one another.

EMBRACE YOUR DIFFERENCES

God has made each of us unique. Best friends tend to celebrate each other's differences. Enemies, on the other hand, use differences as a reason to reject. Do you realize that if you are prejudiced and judgmental toward another person, you can't be that person's friend? That's why the devil loves prejudiced and judgmental people.

Every time we judge someone or act prejudicially toward him or her, we have, in effect, excluded that person from our circle of friends. Yet this is precisely how many people act toward their spouses (and then wonder why there is no sense of friendship in the relationship). Whether through sexism, chauvinism, intellectualism or any other "ism" in which they consider themselves superior, they exclude their spouses from their circle of friends and allow an emotional barrier to be built in the home.

Recently, I counseled a man who, in more than 30 years of marriage, had never experienced an ounce of intimacy in the relationship. After he and his wife had finally begun to work on the problem and make real progress, this is what he told me:

> We've gone to three levels in our relationship. At the first level, we totally *rejected* each other's differences. When we got married, I thought my wife was weird because she preferred to go to bed at a different time than I did, and because she differed from me in what she liked and didn't like. I thought it was my job to change her to be like me. After 10 or 15 years of marriage and total rejection of each other's differences, we got in a huge fight and I realized that was wrong.
>
> Then for about 15 years, we *tolerated* each other's differences. I decided that God had made her the way she was and it was wrong for me to persecute her and try to change her. She was dif-

ferent from me. So I would just live on my side of the house, she could live on her side of the house, and we would share what we could share.

Recently, I've come to understand that we can *celebrate* each other's differences. I am ashamed to say that it has taken me 30 years of marriage to learn this. Because of it, we have never had the intimacy we've desired in our relationship. We don't want to live the rest of our lives this way. Finally, I have come to the place where I can look at her and say, "Thank God for the differences in my wife."

Friends celebrate their differences. They enjoy the fact that each has a gift or a skill that the other doesn't have, or that one person sees things from a different perspective. Our differences can be either dangerous or dynamic in our relationships, depending on how we choose to respond to them and express our feelings about them to our spouses.

If you are going to be best friends with your spouse, there can be no judgment of your mate that says, "There is clearly something wrong with the way God made you, and it's my job to change it. I reject the fact that you're more (or less) sexual. I reject the fact that you're more (or less) emotional. I choose to see your difference from me as a character flaw. Be normal like me."

Enemies say, "I hate those differences in you that don't completely match up with the way that I am." Best friends, however, look at each other appreciatively and say, "Don't we make a great team! We fill in each other's gaps. Look at how we complement one another!"

That's the way best friends think.

BE REAL AND TRANSPARENT

In John 15:15, Jesus said, "No longer do I call you servants, for a servant does not know what his master is doing; but I have called you friends, for all things that I heard from My Father I have made known to you."

The reality behind what Jesus said is a secret to no one: A best friend is someone with whom you don't have to perform. A best friend is real and transparent, and gives you that same right. It's exhausting to be with a person for whom you always have to be "on." It keeps you on edge and you can't relax to be who you truly are. You think, *If I say the wrong thing or do the wrong thing, he (she) is going to reject me.*

With a best friend, you can be real. I'm not talking about being crude or lazy. Your friends, especially your spouse—your very best friend—deserve your best. But he or she is also the one around whom you can be yourself. Jesus said, "I'm calling you my friends. I'm telling you everything the Father told me. I'm opening My heart to you and I'm going to let you be My friends."

I can say anything to Karen, and she can say anything to me. We talk about everything. Your best friend is the person to whom you run when you need to talk. This is the person you pick up the phone to call the moment you receive significant news or experience a life-changing event. If you were standing by yourself and had just received notice on your cell phone that you had won the grand prize in a sweepstakes, the first number you would ring would be your best friend's. That's also the first number you would call if you had just received a doctor's report that you had a terminal illness. Your best friend is your immediate confidant of the information that you possess.

Does what I've just said describe the spirit of your relationship with your wife or your husband? Does your relationship give off a vibe that says, "You can be yourself around me; you can open your heart to me; I'm the safest place"? This is, by the way, the next point. So turn the page and read on!

Notes

1. Kathleen A. Lamb, "Union Formation and Depression: Selection and Relationship Effects," *Journal of Marriage and Family* Vol. 65, Number 4, November 2003, pp. 953-962.
2. Jeffrey S. Gray, "Does Marriage Matter?" quoted in *The Ties that Bind: Perspectives on Marriage and Cohabitation,* ed. Michelle Hindin and Arland Thornton (New York: Aldine de Gruyter, 2000), pp. 356-367.
3. Peggy McDonough, "Chronic Stress and the Social Patterning of Women's Health in Canada" *Social Science and Medicine* Vol. 54, 2002, pp. 767-782.
4. Robert E. Rector, "Marriage: Still the Safest Place for Women and Children," *Heritage Foundation Backgrounder* (Working Paper) Vol. 1732, 2004, pp. 2-3.

CHAPTER 11

Transparency, Fun and Burdens

There are times when a man should be accountable to another Christian man or a woman to another Christian woman, just because they understand each other. But that kind of accountability shouldn't take the place of spouses feeling safe with each other and being able to talk freely with each other about anything they're wrestling with.

BE A PLACE OF REFUGE AND SAFETY

We should be a refuge for our spouses to come and share anything in their lives. The Bible says that Jesus was a friend of sinners—a *friend* of sinners.

Hebrews 4:16 says that because of Jesus we can come boldly before the throne of grace so that we may receive mercy and find grace. Because of God's mercy, not only does He know what you are going through but He also knows the struggles you're going through and why you do what you do. God doesn't just see *what* you do, He sees *why* you do what you do.

One time when I was counseling, I became frustrated with a man who was doing things in the church that were very unhealthy. As I talked with him, though I was kind, I didn't feel a lot of mercy for him, because of what he was doing. Then, in the middle of our conversation, he stopped, looked at me and said, "Pastor Jimmy, I've had 13 step-fathers."

I said, "Excuse me?"

"Between the time I was born and the time I was 18 years old, my mother was married 13 times," he explained. "Since then, I've lost count of all her husbands. Many of those men abused me. A few of them were quite kind to me, but I have been through a lot. I just wanted you to know that before we continued talking."

My attitude instantly changed.

The Bible says that Jesus is merciful. Not only does He know what you are doing, but He also knows your entire history. He knows the pain you've been through, the truths you were not taught as a child, as well as the lies you were taught to believe. He knows the rejection and the heartache. His hand is a good one to take hold of. He's been through all of our temptations, and He went through them without sinning. The Bible tells us that He freely offers us mercy.

He also offers us grace. Grace is a gift—it means having all the free help you need.

We should give grace to our spouses and give whatever support they need to succeed. We need to be thrones of grace for our spouses—providing a place where they can run with their struggles and their mistakes without fear of rejection and judgment.

I have a golfing buddy whose personality is very cut-and-dried in the way he expresses himself. He's "prophetic," and therefore he bluntly tells it just the way he sees it. This especially shows up on the golf course. My golfing partner, Tom, and I play golf with this man and another friend. I always try to take every opportunity to encourage my partner with such words as, "Hey, that was a great shot. You might want to keep your left arm extended a little more. It'll make your next shot even better." My prophetic friend never encourages his partner. One day, his partner turned to him and addressed the issue.

"Why don't you ever encourage me the way Jimmy encourages Tom?"

My friend paused for a moment, said, "Okay,' and then offered this uplifting exhortation: "Try to stop playing so bad."

We all laughed because it's just his personality. But it's a tough personality to live with.

If you're living with someone who doesn't give you a lot of grace, someone who simply is not a very gracious person, ask the Lord, in love, to show you how to bring that relational atmosphere to his or her attention. If you tend to be the one who is judgmental, frank or blunt—ask the Holy Spirit to impart some of His personality to you. His personality is love, joy, peace, patience, kindness, goodness, gentleness, faithfulness and self-control, which is known in the Bible as the fruit of the Spirit (see Gal. 5:22).

The Holy Spirit will loan you His personality at any moment of any day. He's the great mediator (and moderator) of all personality quirks and flaws.

BE FUN, CREATIVE AND POSITIVE

Friendships should be fun. You don't fall in love if you're not having fun.

You become best friends and fall in love by putting some effort into it. When you call each other up and say, "What do you want to do tonight?" you're looking for something you both enjoy doing. You're negotiating an enjoyable atmosphere for building your relationship.

How do you turn a spouse into a friend? Proverbs 18:24 tells us that "a man who has friends must himself be friendly." You have to *be* a good friend to *have* a good friend. You have to purpose to have fun together. Without friendship and fun, marriage is just work. In fact, if you take sex and friendship out of it, marriage is little more than a business relationship.

This may sound a little strange, but Karen and I put effort into having fun in our marriage, and that's what makes our marriage so enjoyable! For example, we celebrated our wedding anniversary recently by going out of town for three days. We stayed in a nice hotel and all we did was have fun. Everything we planned all day long was designed with enjoyment in mind.

There are things we both enjoy and, of course, we do those things. But there are some things that Karen enjoys that aren't necessarily my favorite things to do. (Oh, like seeing girl movies, for example.) But she really likes it when I go see a chick flick with her. She knows I do it purely for her, and it blesses her.

Let me just stop for a moment and explain something about men. We can actually experience something akin to physical pain or an allergic reaction when sitting through *Terms of Endearment* or *The Divine Secrets of the Ya-Ya Sisterhood*. But even when I feel that allergic rash coming on, I do it for Karen, because I love her!

I don't mean to brag or anything, but one time, as a test of endurance, I sat through four "girl" movies in a row. Now, I didn't know in advance that they were all girl movies. Frankly, Karen tricked me.

She said, "Oh, there's a lot of fighting in this one. And it's historical."

The movie? *Sense and Sensibility*, the mother of all three-hanky chick flicks. The good news for me was that there were only two bad parts in the movie—the part where they were talking and the part where they weren't. ("No, honey, I'm not sleeping. I'm just recovering from the exciting parts.")

In the same way, there are things many husbands like to do that their wives find spectacularly uninteresting. But a woman needs to work at being fun for her husband and that may mean going fishing, camping or golfing (or occasionally watching a movie with lots of explosions and car chases).

Both of you must be willing (with a good attitude) to venture out of your world and into your spouse's. You become a selfish fuddy-duddy when you say in effect, "I'm not coming out of my world. If you want someone to go with you to see a girl movie, call a girl! That's why they're called chick flicks. If my friends see me going into that movie, I'll be marked for life!"

Too often in the stable atmosphere of marriage, we stop looking outside the immediate routines of the relationship for new opportunities to have fun. If we keep letting the pressing demands of children and work consume all of our time, before long we'll find that we're no longer having fun together at all.

To find ways to create opportunities for regular fun together, ask yourself what you're passionate about. What does your spouse really like to do? What do you enjoy doing together?

Remember, you'll have many friends, but you'll be best friends with the person with whom you have the most fun. That person should be your spouse.

I love being with Karen. We like walking together—we walk together all the time; we enjoy traveling together—going on trips for two, three or four days several times a year, if we can. And we like sitting on our porch together, talking. We do these things regularly. That's why, when I think about the rest of my life, I think of living it with my best friend. Yes, I love being with my children, and I love other people as well; but I could be with Karen almost exclusively and have a wonderful, contented life. I just like being with her.

It wasn't always that way. And it didn't happen automatically. But today, we have a lot of fun together.

BEAR EACH OTHER'S BURDENS

Karen and I have learned that one of the keys to making a successful marriage is being there for each other. We've discovered that what is burdensome for one of us is not necessarily difficult for the other. Here's a simple example.

Karen is five-foot-five and slender. At one time she had back problems of which the Lord subsequently healed her. I've found that she can easily be worn down by too rigorous a schedule. You see, she wakes up at 4:30 in the morning, has an hour and a half of quiet time, exercises for an hour and a half, and is the hardest worker you'll ever see in your life. She's very diligent. But she simply is not equipped for lifting and carrying things around the house. So I ease her burden by doing all of that kind of thing that I can.

I'm Mr. Tote-It, Fetch-It, Lift-It and Hoist-It at our house.

I go though the house picking things up. I vacuum, carry the groceries in and generally just look for ways to help her with my physical strength. These things are not a burden to me. And they ease what is burdensome for her.

In the same way, running errands around town, such as picking up the dry cleaning, and detail work such as getting the bills paid is burdensome for me. Bill paying is a joyless chore to me. As a result, I would have trouble finding the time to sit down and take care of it. But Karen loves paying the bills. She happily takes care of those kinds of things for me.

What is easy for me can be difficult for Karen, and vice versa. We bear each other's burdens. Why? Because that's what best friends do.

MARRIAGE IS SHARING

Several years ago I counseled a wealthy couple who owned a huge home and literally lived mutually exclusive lives. They very rarely did anything together and thus operated in two completely distinct worlds. They just happened to sleep under the same roof at night. Not surprisingly, in talking with them it became clear that they had no passion, no intimacy and no friendship whatsoever.

What I told them was something simple but profound: "Marriage is about sharing. If you don't share, it's not a marriage."

Marriage is about making decisions together. Marriage is about doing things together. What's really difficult for one person can be easy for two. Let me give you an example.

For many years, Karen and I did our own yard work. Karen enjoyed mowing, and I edged and cleaned up afterwards. We were a team. We loved to go out and work in the yard together. We could easily have done our parts separately, but we enjoyed doing it together. The point is, when Scripture says, "A friend loves at all times, a brother is born for adversity" (Prov. 17:17), it means that a best friend is that person who is there when you need him or her to bear a burden with you or for you. But if you're isolated in your marriage, you aren't there for each other when you need help. This breaks down the bonds that hold the relationship together.

The thought takes root: *I can't count on him* or *She's insensitive to the things that are burdens for me. I'm on my own.*

Karen and I try to be responsive when one or the other of us is under stress. Karen is so great at this. When I'm under a lot of stress preparing to speak or travel, she'll walk in and say, "What can I do for you?" And I'll answer, knowing what she can and cannot do and what she likes and doesn't like to do. Then she does those things for me while I continue my preparation. When I'm out from under the stress of my preparation, I go through the house and do the things that I know are a burden for her. Many times when she comes in the house and goes by the clothes dryer, it's empty and everything is folded. She goes by the dishwasher and it's empty. Everywhere she goes through the house, I've taken care of different things. With every discovery a deposit of love and friendship is made. It's what creates the bond of our relationship.

This is the way we live our lives every day.

To be sure, it wasn't always like that. We had a very different atmosphere in our relationship for quite a while—an atmosphere that wasn't fun and wasn't conducive to friendship. By committing ourselves to each other and to the things that build friendship, we reversed that negative direction. Now you can't separate us.

Maybe you and your spouse were friends at one time but you've lost that aspect of your relationship. You can get it back. Just begin to do those things you did at first. Purposefully commit to taking these steps that may not have been in place before. Your friendship will snap right back.

If you and your spouse got sexual too soon when you first became attracted to each other, or for some other reason you never had a proper courtship period and can't look back on a foundation of friendship, you can begin building one today. It doesn't take very long if you'll just do the things that create an atmosphere that is conducive to friendship. The friendship bond will form. Not only that, but you will also have many years to enjoy the continual growth of that friendship.

Living long and having ever-increasing fun and joy with your best friend is heaven on Earth. It's a taste of paradise in this earthly life.

SECRET FOUR

Be Best Friends

Marriages robbed of friendship
are missing a vital element that
makes that relationship a
paradise. If friendship has
grown cold in your marriage,
or was never given an opportunity
to develop at all, you can
change that.

Ultimate Sexual Fulfillment

The enjoyment of sex, although great
Is in later years said to abate.
This well may be so,
But how would I know?
I'm now only seventy-eight.

Anonymous

CHAPTER 12

Poles Apart

Several decades ago, as the feminist movement began to get traction in this country, it became the orthodoxy within "enlightened" and academic circles to claim that there were no basic differences between men and women. Sure, men could lift heavier stuff, and the plumbing was a little different, but other than that, all the perceived differences in ability and behavior had been culturally ingrained.

In other words, the only reason women behaved differently from men was because little girls were treated differently and were given different toys to play with.

Today, believing that there are no differences between men and women has become so evidently absurd that few people can proclaim it with a straight face. Boys and girls come with different wiring. Men and women simply are different—in very profound and fundamental ways.

Nowhere is the challenge of those differences more evident than in the sexual relationship. I recently read a few suggestions about those differences that I'd like to share with you.

How to Impress a Woman

Wine her
Dine her
Call her
Hug her
Support her

Hold her
Surprise her
Compliment her
Smile at her
Listen to her
Laugh with her
Cry with her
Romance her
Encourage her
Believe in her
Pray with her
Pray for her
Cuddle with her
Shop with her
Give her jewelry
Buy her flowers
Hold her hand
Write love letters to her
Go to the end of the Earth and back again for her

How to Impress a Man

Show up naked
Bring chicken wings
Don't block the TV

It's a joke, of course, but there's a kernel of truth at the center. This tongue-in-cheek list captures the fact that men and women are very different in their sexuality.

Sex was designed by our Creator to be a tremendous blessing in the marriage relationship, but it can also be a source of great tension. Many people marry because of sex; and just as many get divorced because of it.

Our society is obsessed with sex. A quick glance at any magazine rack will reveal scores of cover stories promising to supply tips, techniques and secrets to better sex. Unfortunately, much of the advice we get in our culture about enhancing our sexual experience ignores the true secret to ultimate sex and mutual lasting fulfillment.

Remember, sex was God's idea. He was the one who created it. Just as a thermometer registers the temperature (the environment) within a home, sex can be a type of thermometer within a marriage. Mutual sexual satisfaction shows us something about the relationship. A couple's ability over the long haul to consistently enjoy good sex together reflects their ability to communicate, and it indicates that they're meeting each other's needs and have developed a high level of intimacy. In other words, good sex indicates that other things in the relationship are working.

You can compare the function of sex in marriage not only to a thermometer but also to a thermostat. A thermostat is something that changes the temperature environment of the home to whatever the occupants want it to be. Like a thermostat, good sex makes a marriage better. It is designed to be exclusive to marriage and fulfills its maximum potential only between a husband and wife. Good sex in marriage makes each partner more fond of and drawn to the other in healthy ways.

When a healing, redeeming, mutually esteeming couple has learned how to enjoy being together and how to be best friends—look out! They are poised to discover a secret that is definitely not hidden in Scripture but is certainly a mystery to most of our culture and media. The secret to all sexual fulfillment in marriage is a spirit of servanthood.

THE SEXUALITY OF SERVANTHOOD

You may be thinking, *Servanthood? Jimmy, I know that serving my spouse is important. But I thought the topic was sex, here. I mean, how can a servant spirit be the secret to ultimate sex?*

To answer that question, we need to face some realities regarding our sexuality. The fundamental reality is that none of us can meet our ultimate sexual needs alone. The only way a person's sexual needs can be fully and wholly met is by a member of the opposite sex in the context of marriage. Neither self-pleasure nor promiscuity can meet those needs. *Every* study I've seen has shown that people who are married have better sex than people who are single or living together outside of marriage. So let's establish up front that marriage is the place to have the best sex.

Second, once we're married, we can't force or manipulate our spouses into meeting our sexual needs. We are literally at the mercy of our spouses concerning whether our needs will be met or not. A spouse could withdraw at any point in time, could choose to use sex as a punishment or a weapon—which is devastating to a marriage—or just choose to remain insensitive.

We're simply at each other's mercy. But contrary to our natural instincts, being dependent on someone else is not a bad place to be. We just need to accept the fact that we need each other if we are ever going to experience ultimate sex; and we can't force each other to meet our sexual needs and desires. The challenge, as our humorous lists at the beginning of the chapter illustrated, is that men and women have very divergent sexual needs.

ACCEPTING SEXUAL DIFFERENCES

It is no surprise to anyone who has been married for long that the sexual needs of men and women are different. We differ in nature, intensity and timing. Throughout marriage, our respective sexual needs will ebb and flow. Rarely will they synchronize. Thus, couples will avoid a lot of misdirected energy and frustration by understanding that few, if any, husbands and wives have the same sexual needs.

One general example of this is the fact that men peak sexually in their late teens and early twenties. Women, however, tend to reach their sexual peak in their late thirties or early forties. (Why did God engineer this difference? Probably so that we could have a few years of getting some real work done!)

Men are visually stimulated—they want to "see" their wives. Women are more stimulated when their emotional needs have been met. That's not to say that women are blind to their husbands' bodies; but they're not nearly as visually oriented. (This has led to many a "lights on" versus "lights off" controversy in the bedroom.)

There are other differences. Men can get aroused quite quickly. They don't have to have much foreplay, or even forethought, to be ready for sex. But for women, the turn-on to sex is very gradual. Marriage counselor and author Gary Smalley says that in the world of sex, "men are microwave ovens and women are crock pots." It's true. Women have to warm up to the idea of sex—and it takes awhile.

A man can compartmentalize the sexual experience. He can block everything else out. He could have just had the worst day of his life and been told that tomorrow is Armageddon, and still enjoy sex right now. That's because to him, sex is just another compartment of his life. Not to a woman. A woman is inclusive in her nature. Everything that happens to her is connected to her sexuality. What her husband said to her leaving for work that morning, her interactions with the kids and/or her parents, and the overall condition of their finances is all connected to her sexual responsiveness.

Here's another difference: For a man, sex is a primary need. For a woman, sex is secondary at best. In one study in which men and women were asked to rank how important sex was to them, sex consistently ranked 1, 2 or 3 to men. Women, on average, ranked sex in the number 13 slot—right behind "gardening together," which came in at number 12. That's right, in the average woman's hierarchy of things to do with her husband, sex takes a backseat to pulling weeds.

There are more differences. But the ones I've mentioned are enough to make the point: Men and women are different in nature and in need when it comes to sex.

DON'T BASE SEX ON MUTUAL DESIRE

With such wide-ranging differences in priority, intensity and timing, it's clear that we must base our sexual fulfillment on something more than mutual desire. If we're always waiting for our spouse to have the same sexual needs at the same time we do, we're going to spend a lot of time waiting. Rarely are we going to have the same needs at the same time.

For that reason, there must be a spirit of servanthood in the marriage relationship. This was no secret in the first paradise. Sex was God's idea. Adam and Eve were wired for ultimate sexual fulfillment. They could have had the ultimate sex, because God created them to serve Him and serve each other. They were helpmates in the Garden.

But they sinned and lost the paradise of their marriage. Do you remember that one of their first responses when sin came into their relationship was to cover themselves with fig leaves? Their sexuality was separated, withheld from each other, the moment they sinned, because the essence of the sin of mankind is to reject servanthood to God and others.

SERVANTS LIVE TO PLEASE

Sin has made serving one another seem much more complicated than it really is. That was evident when a lawyer, who was testing Jesus, asked, "Teacher, which is the great commandment in the Law?" (Matt. 22:36).

Jesus answered, "'You shall love the LORD your God with all your heart, with all your soul, and with all your mind.' This is the first and great commandment. And the second is like it: 'You shall love your neighbor as yourself.' On these two commandments hang all the Law and the Prophets" (vv. 37-40).

The two greatest commandments are a response to man's greatest needs—to serve God and to serve other people. Serving others is the essence of why we were created. That's why many servants are much happier than their masters—they live to please another person, not to please themselves. This is the way man is designed. It's why government employees—from the police officer to the president—are called public servants. It's why a successful employee seeks ways to help serve the vision and goals of the business he works for. And it's why business owners succeed not by hard work alone but by making sure their businesses serve the needs of their customers.

If your goal is to please other people, you can do that all day long and be successful at it. But if you live to please yourself, you have taken on an impossible task. Like a dog chasing its tail, self-satisfaction is impossible to find when that is what you live for.

Man was created to serve. All fulfillment in life comes from being a servant.

THE MASTER WHO SERVED

Jesus demonstrated the height of servanthood with His life and death. He brought serving to the forefront after the Last Supper with His disciples:

> And supper being ended . . . Jesus, knowing that the Father had given all things into His hands, and that He had come from God and was going to God, rose from supper and laid aside His garments, took a towel and girded Himself. After that, He poured water into a basin and began to wash the disciples' feet, and to wipe them with the towel with which He was girded.
>
> Then He came to Simon Peter. And Peter said to Him, "Lord, are You washing my feet?" Jesus answered and said to him, "What I am doing you do not understand now, but you will know after this." Peter said to Him, "You shall never wash my feet!" Jesus answered him, "If I do not wash you, you have no part with Me . . ."
>
> When He had washed their feet, taken His garments, and sat down again, He said to them, "Do you know what I have done to you? You call me Teacher and Lord, and you say well, for so I am. If I then, your Lord and Teacher, have washed your feet, you also ought to wash one another's feet. For I have given you an example, that you should do as I have done to you. Most assuredly, I say to you, a servant is not greater than his master; nor is he who is sent greater than he who sent him. If you know these things, blessed are you if you do them" (John 13:2-8,12-17).

Jesus constantly taught (and modeled) servanthood. Fast-forward a few days from the incident described above to the time when the disciples went back to the Sea of Galilee after Jesus was resurrected (see John 21).

When they returned from a fruitless night of fishing on the lake, they found Jesus on the shore cooking them breakfast. This was the glorified, resurrected King of kings—fixing breakfast for a band of stinky fishermen!

Jesus didn't serve people only when He was on the earth. The Bible tells us that He is an eternal servant (see Rom. 8:34). Our Lord finds joy in serving, as demonstrated by His words: "Come to Me, all you who labor and are heavy laden, and I will give you rest. Take My yoke upon you and learn from Me, for I am gentle and lowly in heart, and you will find rest for your souls" (Matt. 11:28-29).

God's spirit is a servant spirit. When you choose to demonstrate a servant spirit toward others, you are demonstrating a kindred spirit with God's. It's the secret of all fulfillment in life.

SUPERIOR POSITION—SERVANT HEART

A lot of people associate a servant or servant spirit with someone of low rank and importance. But from a heavenly perspective, the opposite is true. What Jesus not only taught but also demonstrated was that servanthood is a superior, not an inferior, spirit that acts out of faith and confidence and produces powerful results. In God's system of government, those who possess a servant spirit are regarded as the highest in rank and most worthy of honor.

Look again at the description we just read of Jesus' washing of the disciples' feet: "Jesus, knowing that the Father had given all things into His hands, and that He had come from God and was going to God, rose from supper and laid aside His garments, took a towel and girded Himself." Jesus knew that He had come from God and that He was going back to God. He knew that God had put everything into His hands. And knowing all that, He stood up and served.

Selfishness springs from weakness and fear; and dominance and manipulation actually stem from a sense of insecurity. But true servanthood springs from a sense of security and confidence and power.

Jesus knew who He was, where He was going, and that the universe was His. Secure in that knowledge, He was free to kneel down and wash the dirty feet of His followers.

Do you remember what the disciples were talking about during that time? We know from the record of Luke 22 that the disciples were having a debate about who was the greatest among them. It was in the middle of that discussion that Jesus shocked them all by washing their feet. Peter was so shocked that he insisted, "You shall never wash my feet!" That's when Jesus said, "If I do not wash you, you have no part with Me." In other words, "If you're not willing to associate with Me as a servant, you have no part in Me. You cannot be a part of what I am about to do."

The world's way is to be served; God's way is to serve. The world's way teaches us to focus on our own needs; God's way teaches us to focus on other people's needs.

Nowhere is this principle of servanthood more at work than within the marriage relationship.

CHAPTER 13

Free from the Fear of Servanthood

The biblical principle of serving your spouse may be totally different from the counsel you expected to receive about getting to a place of ultimate sexual fulfillment. In fact, you may even be thinking, *This is not going to work in my situation. If I start serving my spouse, he (she) will just take advantage of me.*

One of the greatest fears among wives (and among quite a few husbands), involves the fear of what will happen if they serve their spouses wholeheartedly and unreservedly. I can understand this fear.

Early in our marriage, I was very dominant. Karen and I did not have a rich, intimate sex life. I've already described how I was verbally abusive to her and how I was basically a jerk and didn't pay attention to her needs. And though my heart's desire was for us to have meaningful physical intimacy and great sex, that just wasn't the case.

Karen was certainly faithful to meet my sexual needs. She didn't punish me by withholding sex or ever use it as a weapon. But we were not truly intimate and didn't achieve the level of sexual fulfillment I longed for.

Then I changed.

I repented—to Karen and to God—for being such a jerk. I began to humble myself and serve Karen as best I could. At first, I did it with the lingering fear that I was going to be a male maid around the house. I thought, *She's going to work me to death and I'll see nothing for it.*

I'm sure that I'm not the only spouse who has ever had those thoughts. So let's deal with the misconceptions that give birth to those fears.

LOSS OF POSITION?

First of all, serving is an act of love and faith for another person. You don't give up your position when you serve. Jesus, the servant, rebuked the man whose feet He was washing. When Jesus began to wash Peter's feet, and Peter took issue with Him, Jesus rebuked him. He could not have done that if, by taking the servant role, He had automatically surrendered His leadership position.

You don't give up your position when you serve. A man may try to reinforce his position as head of the house by insisting, "Well, I'm the man of the house, and I don't need to serve my wife; I need to be served. I'm afraid if I start serving her and meeting her desires, it will mean that she's ruling me."

When a man serves his wife, she is not ruling him. He still has authority, but that authority is exercised and expressed through service. This kind of authority is God-given and is most like Christ's. Authority that would enforce itself through dominance is ungodly authority that will never draw from another person what is desired.

When we're too proud to serve, we're saying, *I'm going to get what I want through pride, dominance, manipulation and coercion. I believe that has more power than humility and grace.*

That's the approach I tried in my home for many years. All it did for me was drive my wife further away from me emotionally, physically and in every other way. But when I began to serve Karen, for the first time in our marriage, I truly established my authority. Today I am the servant leader of our home. I am the head servant.

You may be saying, *Pastor Jimmy, it's fine for you to talk about becoming the servant leader and head servant. But I can't make another person serve me. I don't have any guarantee my spouse is going to reciprocate.*

No, you can't force your spouse to join you in taking on that servant spirit, but you can sure lead by example. A basic principle we've already looked at is that the only way you can defeat a spirit is with the opposite spirit. If you feel that your spouse is selfish, you will never defeat that spirit with more selfishness. You will only defeat it through servanthood.

Let me put it another way. When both of you are waiting on the other to serve, all you have is two selfish people at a standoff. You've got a bad marriage. But even if you are the only one to take the position of servant in your marriage, you are much farther along than you were when both of you were at a standoff.

Someone always has to make the first move toward paradise. If you feel as if your spouse isn't listening, doesn't care, isn't meeting your sexual needs, how do you deal with that? You make the first move by choosing a heart of service.

Jesus made the first move at the Last Supper. He had 12 men at the table with Him—12 guys who had a history of selfish ambition and jockeying for position. Yet it was Jesus, the one in the superior position, who got up from the table and washed their feet. Not only did He have the superior position, but He also had the superior spirit.

Jesus' act of humility and service was so profound that it shocked the disciples and started a movement that changed history and continues to change hearts and lives today.

If you think your marriage isn't working, then consider what you can do to change it. You may have tried pride. You may have tried dominance, manipulation, punishment by withdrawal, rejection. But you and I both know that these behaviors only leave a trail of divorce, damaged lives and relational devastation across all strata of our culture. Servanthood, however, never fails. Servanthood leaves restoration in its path.

BE FIRST TO DO THE RIGHT THING

Here's my best advice for single people who are looking for a marriage partner: Commit to being a servant and look for a servant to marry. When you find one another, you'll have the makings of a good marriage from the very beginning. Look for that person who has a heart to do the right thing first. But don't wait for him or her to act. Instead, commit to being the one who acts first.

Taking action first is so key to a healthy marriage. The "best" person always does the right thing first. So even if you're the one who's right and your spouse is in the wrong, if you're the best person in the marriage—

meaning that you're the one who cares most about making the marriage better—you will serve your spouse. And you won't lose any authority when you take that position.

Set aside the fear that causes you to think you will lose your rights if you stoop to wash the feet of your spouse. Don't say to yourself, *I would serve my spouse, but I don't want to be controlled.* That's wrong thinking. The truth is that you will have more influence from a position of service.

A Marriage Saved by Serving

A woman who ultimately came to be a part of our ministry wrote the following testimony of what happened in her marriage when she brought a servant spirit into the bedroom:

Dear Jimmy,

My husband has gone through a very difficult time for the past three years due to hurts he has experienced from people in almost every area of his life. Over a period of time, the enemy managed to pile one hurt on top of another, causing great emotional trauma and emotional anger. During this time, our relationship became strained, and I became the enemy along with almost every person in his life. Nothing I did was acceptable to him, because the enemy had been so successful inflicting deep wounds.

One day, the Lord spoke to me very clearly that the only open door to his spirit was through sex. He said that I needed to be very careful to keep that door open. My husband wasn't particularly appealing to me at that time because anger infected every word and facial expression, and I was well aware of his feelings toward me. Still, the Lord's words rang in my spirit. I knew that it was a strong warning to me that if I wasn't obedient, there would be devastating consequences that could not be undone.

As a result, God has done the miraculous in our lives and has been faithful in our marriage to go beyond restoration. I can't adequately describe the strength in our relationship. It is simply amazing.

As a side note, there is still healing in other relationships that needs to take place, but I know it will. We serve the most awesome, loving God. I take no credit for this. It was only by the goodness and grace of God that I was able to heed the warning and follow it. I know this is a powerful key in the spirit realm, one with profound ramifications.

This couple is active in our ministry, and I know them well. The wife chose to deal with the attack on their relationship by doing what I've been describing. She chose to exercise a redemptive spirit. She chose to be a servant to her husband at the point of his need. By doing so, she rescued him and she saved their marriage.

CHAPTER 14

Sweet Sweat

Serving your spouse is a powerful weapon in the battle to restore and strengthen your marriage. This spiritual truth has even shown up in some interesting scientific research. For example, every guy needs to know about the results of a rather unusual study of women's reactions conducted at the University of Pennsylvania. Research psychologists there gathered a group of women on the premise they would be testing cosmetics and household products.[1]

What these women were really testing was something totally different. The testers applied a substance they said was a household product on the women's upper lips. When the substance had been applied under their noses, they were each asked to note how they felt. The most common responses were, "I feel relaxed," "I feel happy," "I feel sexually aroused."

Do you know what had been applied to the upper lips of those women?

Pheromones from male sweat!

The testers rubbed the essence of male perspiration on the women's upper lips, and the women felt more relaxed, happier and sexually aroused. Isn't it interesting that God has wired women in such a way that the result of hard physical effort turns them on? May I state the obvious? What a wife needs is to see her husband working around the house!

In another study, this one conducted by the University of Washington, women were asked, "When is your husband most sexually attractive to you?"[2]

The number one response: "When he's doing housework." I tell you, men, if you want to appeal to your wives, don't flex your biceps—grab a vacuum cleaner and work up a sweat! That's right, service is sexy.

This is also true for women. Men delight to see their wives serving. It's a major key to our sexuality.

Obviously, men and women have been giving attention to the wrong thing. Many men and women are putting most of their effort and money into trying to be more beautiful, more handsome, more buff. And certainly, physical attractiveness is important. Others are giving their whole focus to sexual technique. And that can help, too. But neither working on physical appearance nor improving sexual technique is the real issue.

If the physical stuff were all that mattered, the "beautiful people" in Hollywood would have the greatest sex and the greatest marriages possible. But they have some of the worst of both! At the time I was writing this, two high-profile film stars were going through an on again-off again engagement after buying a million-dollar engagement ring. Here were two of the most beautiful people on Earth, with the greatest "chemistry" and the money to do the most romantic things imaginable—and they couldn't get along. Though such celebrities may be living in a material paradise, very few have discovered paradise in their marriages. That's because the best sex is between two servants.

MEETING THE NEEDS OF ANOTHER

A servant is constantly sensitive to the needs of another. Consider the Last Supper once again. Thirteen men were sitting at the table, but only one person was aware of anyone else's needs. With the exception of Jesus, every other man at that table was aware only of his own agenda.

Rarely will two people have the same level of sexual need at the same time. Add to that a marriage in which both husband and wife are acting out of independent and selfish spirits, and you create a recipe for sexual frustration and marital disaster. You have a totally different situation when husband and wife operate in a spirit of servanthood. A servant thinks, *I wonder if she (he) needs anything?* That's the way a servant is trained. A servant's pleasure is in seeing another person's pleasure realized.

FROM SERVANT TO SEXUALLY FULFILLED

Once we see the absolute necessity of having a servant spirit in the sexual relationship, the question that remains is, *How do I get from servanthood to a point of ultimate sexual fulfillment?*

That pathway is an upward journey of higher and higher mutual gratification. Let's look at the five levels of meeting needs in a relationship.

Level five: All needs are being unmet. At this level, both husband and wife are completely distracted and insensitive to any needs but their own.

Level four: Some needs are being met. This stage characterizes a couple that is committed to each other, but they're compromised. When you ask how many of their needs are being met, each would say some needs are being met but many are not. This stage indicates that there is some insensitivity in the relationship. Neither spouse is serving or loving the other.

Level three: Basic needs are being met. A partner would describe the satisfaction level at this stage of their relationship as, "Yes, my basic needs are being met, but I have a lot of dreams, desires and needs that are not being met right now." Again, though committed to one another, this husband and wife are limited in the extent to which each is meeting the needs of the other.

Level two: All needs are being met. This husband or wife would say there is no unmet need in the relationship. They are not only committed, but they are also sensitive to one another's every need. In my commitment to Karen, she only has to whisper her need one time—in fact, I don't even want her to have to tell me. I have spent 30 years studying her. I'm an expert. I've got a Ph.D. in Karen. I'm paying attention. I don't even want her to have to say it before I'm able to do it. That's what it means to be sensitive to and to serve somebody. What I tell Karen is, "Till my death, I'll meet your needs."

Level one: Not only all needs, but also all desires, are being met. By "desire," I don't mean sinful lusts or cravings. I'm talking about God-given desires based on His Word and on our unique personalities. It's possible to have every need met yet still have unrealized desires, dreams and hopes. Psalm 37:4 says, "Delight yourself also in the LORD, and He shall give you the desires of your heart." God is not just a God who meets your needs; He also cares about your desires.

PARADISE—A PLACE OF DESIRE

Paradise is not just a place where our basic needs are met. It is a place of fulfilled desire—a place where two people live fully to please each other. Our desires are never going to be realized until another person freely and willingly chooses to help fulfill them.

Think about it: If we could meet our own needs sexually (or in any other area), we wouldn't get married. The reason we get married is because it's the only place where sexual needs can be healthily fulfilled. But that fulfillment is totally dependent upon one's spouse. If our spouse is insensitive, we're in trouble. If our spouse is uncommitted, we're in trouble. If our spouse has a limited level of commitment demonstrated by thinking that goes, *Well, I'm going to take care of your basic needs, but beyond that you had just better be happy,* then there's trouble in paradise.

It's a pretty simple concept: Husbands and wives need each other.

Thus, when two people in a marriage unreservedly serve one other, they have a prescription for paradise. Paradise is a place that you cannot find without a servant spirit. You will never arrive there without two people sharing an attitude based on thinking that says, *I live for your pleasure. I'm not just here to take care of your basic needs. I'm not just here to give you meat and broccoli. I'm here to give you cake and pie, sugar and sweets, until your teeth rot out!*

That is the secret to ultimate sexual fulfillment—a servant's spirit. As soon as you live to serve your spouse, you're on your way to sexual fulfillment.

TAKE THE SUPERIOR POSITION

Even if you're the only one in the relationship doing anything about it, you have the key to ultimate sex in your possession. Don't lose that key by giving in to fear that says, *If I serve my wife, she'll work me to death* or *If I serve my husband, he'll try to control me.* I can assure you that over the long haul that is not going to happen.

Husband, when you begin to serve your wife, you're going to get a response from her that you've never seen before. When she smells some of that sweat on you, man, you've had it! You just need to sweat more. I'm talking about sweating in her service by helping around the house.

Wife, use your sexuality, your gift of sex. Use that gift even if he's distracted or tends toward rejection or withdrawal in his communication with you. The gift of sex is an incredibly powerful gift that God has given women to serve and meet the needs of their husbands.

Not only can husbands and wives turn around the lives of their spouses and their marriages, but they can also lead the way into the paradise of relational fulfillment simply by serving one another.

In the next chapter, I will provide specific and practical ways that you can make this paradise happen.

Notes

1. Terence Monmaney and Susan Katz, "The Chemistry Between People: Are Our Bodies Affected by Another Person's Scent?" *Newsweek,* January 12, 1987.
2. Sarah Womack, "Housework Gives Men Sex Appeal: Study," *The Age,* August 23, 2003. http://www.theage.com.au/articles/2003/08/27/1061663849774.html (accessed February 2006).

CHAPTER 15

Seven Sexual Secrets for Men

Men, once you are committed to demonstrate a servant spirit toward your wife, you will want to apply some very practical behavior to your efforts. (I'll speak to the women in the following chapter!)

I strongly encourage you to consider the following seven points of advice regarding your wife's sexual needs. If you do so and make some necessary changes, I promise that you will serve your wife better and she will respond.

1. Prepare for your wife's menstrual cycle.

I wish that someone had given me this advice years ago. Keep track of your wife's menstrual cycle and mentally prepare yourself for it. You might even want to make sure your medicine cabinet is always stocked with what I call A.T.M.—anti-terrorist medicine—more commonly known as menstrual pain relief medication!

A woman's natural monthly menstrual cycle makes a dramatic difference in her sexual response. Obviously, during her period there's an issue you have to deal with. But you also need to be aware of when ovulation occurs. A woman ovulates between her menstrual cycles, and ovulation is the time when she's normally the most sexual and the most open to sex. However, it certainly doesn't mean it's the only time she's sexual.

You also need to be aware that before she starts her period, she often experiences bloating and tremendous sensitivity in her breasts and other parts of her body, possibly including her female organs. This can cause her to feel irritable. The important thing for you to know is that her irritability is not rejection. Many guys feel rejected and frustrated because they just don't understand these monthly changes in their wife's body, so they don't prepare for this reality. A woman's body is much more hormonally complex than a man's. She will respond emotionally and sexually in different ways throughout the month in relation to the timing of her menstrual cycle that month.

2. Be sensitive to every problem and stress your wife is experiencing.

As men, we tend to compartmentalize the different facets of our lives. We can have a horrible day at the office and not have it affect our desire for sex that night. Women do not compartmentalize; they synthesize. That means that *everything* in a woman's life matters to her and affects her sexual response. That means that every event of the day and every facet of life factors into her mood and receptiveness.

For example, you need to be a good financial partner and planner. But don't dominate the finances. Karen and I manage the finances together. I do most of the investing and financial planning, but I include Karen in every decision as my partner. Karen balances the checkbook because she's good at it and enjoys it. While I take the financial burden off of her shoulders for the bigger picture decisions, I make sure that we both understand and agree about what's going on.

Because a woman's sexual responses are impacted by what happens in every area of her life, it's important that you take time to talk with your wife before sex. Ask if anything is bothering her. Find out if there is anything she needs to talk about. Sitting down with your wife and talking with her about her problems, fears and concerns helps her to be receptive to you. Unlike you, she can't compartmentalize areas of her life that aren't going so well and just head off to bed.

When you do what's right with the children and take an active role in their care, your actions release your wife's spirit. She needs to know that you love the children, that you're paying attention to them, and that you're disciplining them properly. She needs to know that you're fulfilling your position as spiritual leader in the family, which takes a tremendous burden off of her and opens her up to you. The fact is, the deepest intimacy you can share is spiritual intimacy. So pray with your wife. Be the priest of your home. Take on the spiritual leadership.

And don't try to do dirty things in bed—things that are just wrong. There are wide parameters for great sex, but there's no place for dirty things. It's important that you take spiritual leadership in the bedroom as well as every other area of your marriage.

Be there physically for your wife to serve and support her. Help around the house and make sure that she knows you're serving around the house. Nothing turns on wives more than connected, servant husbands.

3. Be sensitive to the characteristics of her nature.

Just because your wife's sexual responses probably do not match yours doesn't mean that she doesn't need sex. Nevertheless, her four major needs are security, open and honest communication, nonsexual affection and leadership. These needs are indeed greater for her than her need for sex.

Too many men try to change their wives, hoping to get their wives to be as sexual as they are. Your wife is simply not going to be as sexually motivated as you, but you can definitely put her in touch with her sexuality by meeting her emotional needs. Make her feel secure. Talk to her the way you should, hold her in a nonsexual way—giving her soft, nonsexual affection. And be the loving leader—not dominant, but taking loving initiative. That's what meets your wife's emotional needs and opens her up sexually. That's the way God made her.

4. Be romantic.

Focus on your wife's needs, not yours. While romance may end in sex, to your wife, sex and romance are not synonymous or even necessarily linked. Romance can mean cards and flowers and taking her out to some place special for some quality time with you. And you plan and initiate this. In other words, romance is all the ways in which you can cause a woman to think, *I'm on his heart. He's thinking about me and giving attention to me when he doesn't have to. I'm special to him.*

In contrast, an unromantic husband is one you would have to whack on the head to get his attention. His failure to give any thought or focus to what his wife cares about causes her to come to only one conclusion:

He doesn't think about me. He only pays attention to me when I'm nagging, when I'm right in his face. But if I weren't there, he wouldn't think about me at all. That's a total turnoff to a woman. It's anti-romance.

What your wife wants to know is that she's desirable. She wants to hear by your actions and your thoughtfulness: *You're desirable to me. You are so desirable to me that when I'm away from you, I'm still desiring you. And these roses and this card are just a token to you of how desirable you are to me.* When she knows that, she's in heaven.

5. Be sensitive to her sexual responses.

While orgasm in sex is not optional for us guys, it is optional for our wives. They can have sex without necessarily having an orgasm. If a man doesn't have an orgasm, he thinks, *What's the point?* But when your wife tells you she doesn't have to have an orgasm to have good sex, that's what she means. When a woman needs and wants an orgasm, it's something that takes more effort. Bringing her to that point takes a lot more communication and sensitivity than it does for a man.

In general, women are less sexual than men. That's not true for every couple, nor does it need to be. In those cases in which the woman is more sexual than the husband, the husband needs to meet her needs. The Bible is clear on this.

The reason a man needs to be aware that in most cases he is more sexual than his wife is to avoid feeling rejected and having the expectation that his wife should naturally be as sexually ready as he is.

For years, I didn't understand this. Karen said to me many times, "Jimmy, you know, I want to meet your sexual needs. And I'm committed to it. But you have to understand, I don't sit around thinking about sex all the time."

I thought, *How strange you are, woman. You must need deliverance. Why aren't you thinking about sex?* The fact is that women generally do not spend nearly the amount of time thinking about sex that men do. So it's not something that, as a husband, you should feel rejected about or should try to change. It is, however, something that you can give attention to and cause her to open up to by first meeting her emotional needs.

Women are less visually stimulated in sexual ways. Though our wives want us to be attractive, fit and well groomed, they just don't have the same visual orientation that we do. Just do what she says and believe her, and meet her needs on her level. She's different sexually from you—in a big way.

6. Be pure in your thoughts and actions.

Pornography fills our media. I'm not just referring to what is being shown on late-night subscription channels. Regular TV broadcast programming throughout the day is filled with pornography. What is being shown is absolutely horrendous, and it saturates our society.

Sexually oriented dating shows that air during the family programming hours suggest that there are women out there who don't have emotional needs and who are not nearly as complicated as your wife—women who are wired for sex and don't require you to meet any emotional needs. Let me correct that suggestion right now. A man who would marry any one of those contestants would discover the same thing any other married man has discovered—that women—*all women*—have emotional needs that are very different from a man's.

If someone were to marry that "sexually wired" date contestant, things would be very different. Women are not like the TV portrayals or the fantasies some are trying to project. Those are lies straight from the pit of hell. And a husband who would try to compare his wife to that kind of portrayal is headed for marital frustration and disaster. There is no way a wife can perform to fulfill that "instant turn-on, always ready for sex" fantasy. And no husband who leaves his wife is going to find it in real life.

Men, especially those who travel and stay in hotel rooms, are viewing pornography and then trying to get their wives to act out what they see on the "adult" and pay-per-view porn channels. But a good woman won't do it. A good woman will be very sexual and serve her husband and meet his sexual needs in an energetic and creative way, but she is going to resist the porn-driven activity, because it's wrong. It's wrong to allow that stuff into your mind and into your bedroom. Purity is what creates the best sex.

7. Be prayerful about your sexual problems and unmet sexual needs.

The way to deal with your sexual problems and your unmet sexual needs is to turn them over to God. Pray, "Lord, my sexual needs are not getting met." Or "Lord, I'm lusting. I'm having a problem with pornography." You can't get the problem fixed until you go to God. Whatever your need is, God's throne is a throne of grace.

Understand that God is not ashamed of you. The Bible says that Jesus can sympathize with our weaknesses because He was tempted in every way that we are, yet was without sin (see Heb. 4:15). Jesus knows what it's like to be attacked in the area of sexuality. He was a man for many years on this Earth. He lived in His sexual prime, as a single man, without ever sinning.

Gentlemen, do you know what that means for us? We can go before God and pray, "God, please help my wife to understand me sexually. Please help me to understand my wife. I pray that You would help me deal with the thoughts I am thinking, the battles I am going through." When you turn toward God, you turn to the One who created sex. He's the only One who can bring us to fulfillment in this area of our lives.

I know many churches that have ministries to help men who have sexual addictions. It's amazing to see what the devil can do to a man. They come into the sexual addiction classes having had more sexual experience at younger ages than most people have in their entire lives. When you're living that way, it's all that you're living for.

These men are dead—they're dead in their eyes and in their spirits. Many have lost their families, their jobs and their fortunes. One man had credit card bills for $70,000 for Internet pornography and had lost three wives because of pornography. I'm telling you, these are not fulfilled men. They are dead men walking.

Men, you must stay pure and turn these kinds of temptations over to God. You must understand that your wife is different from you and needs a servant leader in order for her life to be fulfilled and for her to reach her sexual potential as your partner.

CHAPTER 16

Seven Sexual Secrets for Women

Just as there are practical ways for husbands to better serve their wives sexually, wives can do specific things to prepare them to meet their husband's sexual needs.

1. Let your husband know that you accept his sexual nature as valid and God-given.

Sex is a primary need for a man. And as such, it is a doorway into his spirit and his emotions. Don't reject that part of him. You should no more reject his thinking often about sex any more than he should judge you for not thinking about it often.

And men do think about sex—a lot. That's the way God made them. He did it to lead husbands back to their wives and homes—to be connected there, to be fulfilled there. So don't call your husband names that depict his sexual desire in a negative light. And don't treat him as if he wants sex too much. You have to understand that when he comes to you for sex, God gave him that desire to keep him coming back to you. To reject him for it is to work against the nature of God in him.

2. Be creative and energetic in meeting his sexual needs and desires.

Your husband's pleasure is your pleasure. So don't allow yourself to get in a rut. You're in a rut if you wear the same sleepwear every night. You're in a rut if you limit yourself to just meeting your husband's basic sexual needs. Be creative. Study what your husband likes and what he wants.

Find out what his desires are sexually and serve him in that area. It's the most powerful thing in the world for a man to know that his wife is not just willing to meet a basic need but is willing to meet the need he wants.

One area to consider is what your husband likes visually. A man's visual stimulation tends to collide with the fact that most women don't like their own bodies. In fact, the lowest self-esteem of any women's group in America is among fashion models. And it's all because of comparison. Men do some comparing of other men, but they aren't nearly as affected by it.

Women are obsessed with comparison. It causes them to immediately become self-conscience about specific parts of their bodies. Whether a woman is self-conscious about her hips, breasts, legs or whatever else, she looks at every other woman and compares herself.

To make things worse, television and magazines constantly put seemingly perfect bodies on display. When you get through looking at those bodies, it's difficult not to look at yourself in the mirror and think, *This is gross. What is this body compared to what I just saw on television? Why would I want to put this in a spotlight by putting on lingerie? I want to cover this baby up with some heavy denim fabric and tape the windows shut!*

What society's perception has done to women is tragic. Women should not have to perform like that. I'm 49, and Karen is a bit younger, but both of our bodies have changed. I decided long ago that I would never compare Karen to another woman. I have always told her that she is attractive to me, even during the times she has gained weight. (With both pregnancies, she gained 50 pounds.) But I consistently told her she was always attractive to me. I have never criticized her for her looks—especially through the changes wrought by having babies and aging.

Why would I compare my wife's body to someone who hasn't paid the price to bear my children? Yes, I'm visual. I like to see her naked. And she's more attractive to me today than ever.

For a woman to meet her husband's sexual needs, she has to do things that are somewhat unnatural to her. For instance, women would not naturally put on lingerie, but men enjoy it. At a marriage seminar I led years ago in Pennsylvania, there was a would-be standup comedian in the audience. When I said to the women, "Ladies, there is a place for flannel nightgowns," he yelled, "Yeah, the fireplace!" All I'm saying is be sensitive to your husband's sexual nature.

A man's number-one need is honor. His ego is extremely sensitive, and it's totally connected to his sexuality. So honor your husband. Treat him like you would the Lord. His second highest need is sex. His third is kindred fellowship. He wants to have fun with you. Don't mother him; be his friend. Find ways to have fun with your husband. His fourth highest need is domestic support. Use the gift of turning your house into a home. Use it very carefully, because it's an important need for men. That doesn't mean wives should do all the housework; husbands can and should be equal partners in it. That's what I do with my wife, but I deeply appreciate the tremendous gift Karen has of turning our house into a home.

4. Be romantic.

Romance for a man means sex. Order pizza and get naked, and he's in heaven. That's about it. The only thing better is if there's a football game afterwards. I'm telling you, pizza, sex and football. It doesn't get much better than that for a guy. But just as I encourage husbands to learn the language of romance their wives appreciate, wives need to find ways to be romantic toward their husbands in the language guys understand. Don't try to romance him in your language; that just frustrates him. There's too much talking, and it takes too long!

5. Be organized about sex.

Woman can have better sex if they plan it in advance. Men can be very spontaneous—just plan to take care of the kids. In fact, if you know he's going to want sex that night, it's helpful when your husband comes in from work to tell him what you plan and what you need: "Honey, I want to really give you some good sex tonight. I want to tell you that right up front. But here's what I need from you. I need you to clean the kitchen . . . take care of the kids . . ." Just tell him what you need, but be organized about it.

When our children were still at home, Karen and I would say to each other, "Are we going to be together tonight?" It was our code for "Are we planning a night for sex?" And Karen would say, "Yeah, let's be together," or "No, Jimmy, let's be together tomorrow night." She knew to plan the day around it.

When your husband comes in from work, tell him what you need from him so that you can be free to go take a bath, rest or do whatever you need to do to be sexually responsive.

6. Be sexual.

Act sexier than you feel. God has given you a powerful gift, and it's something you can use whenever you need to use it. Don't let your identity be smothered in being a mother, by being a career person or by any other role. When you're around your husband, remember that he needs you to be sexual for him. He needs you to think sexual, look sexual and act sexual. Many times you won't feel sexual at all, but you can be more sexual than you feel because it's a very important thing to your husband.

7. Be honest.

Communicate to your husband what you like and don't like. Sometimes women don't communicate what they want sexually, due perhaps to a feeling of shame, awkwardness or a real sense of modesty. When you don't communicate, your husband will be totally frustrated. Many men truly want to please their wives, but they don't know how.

Of course there's a wrong way to communicate. What's really demoralizing for a man is when the only way his wife communicates is through negatives: "I don't like that" or "Don't do that."

What your husband needs to know is what you *do* like. What is it that you would enjoy? What could he do for you that would really help you to enjoy sex? And you need to be clear about it, because communicating about sex and getting it out in the open is the only way you can meet each other's needs.

Karen and I talk about this. It's a major topic of our vision retreats every year. We ask each other, "Are you fulfilled? Is there anything that I need to change?" When we come out of that time together, we know how each other feels and that we're meeting each other's sexual needs and desires. As a result, we have a great sex life.

Regardless of what you know, regardless of anything I have written in the way of practical advice or about understanding the differences between men and women, don't lose sight of that primary secret to ultimate sex: *Ultimate sex begins with a servant spirit.* It begins with an attitude that says, "Your pleasure is my pleasure. I am living to please you. I'm studying you because I'm dedicated like a servant to his (her) master to please you."

I'm not talking about giving up your equality in the relationship. I'm talking about your representing your position from an attitude of service, just as Jesus served you. It is from that position that you and your mate will be able to experience the marriage God wants you to have.

Ultimate Sexual Fulfillment

The position of servanthood—
modeled by both of you—opens
the door to ultimate sex in your
secret paradise.

The Serpent Expelled

Who first seduced them to that foul revolt?
The infernal Serpent; he it was whose guile,
Stirred up with envy and revenge, deceived
The mother of mankind.

John Milton, *Paradise Lost*

CHAPTER 17

The Real Enemy

I mentioned at the beginning of this journey that in order to discover the path to paradise, we would have to go all the way back to the original couple in the original paradise—the Garden of Eden.

As you've begun to receive insights into God's plan for restoring paradise to your marriage, I hope you have also begun to see that these barriers to a strong, happy marriage are not rooted in your spouse or in you. To turn your marriage around, you must know how to slam the door shut on the one who ruined that paradise in the first place. The question thus becomes: *How can we have a serpent-free paradise?*

For the answer, we must look at God's original intent for marriage and at what happened to cause that first marriage to become separated from the paradise it was designed to enjoy. You see, God put Adam and Eve in the Garden of Eden, and it was His plan for them to enjoy it always. They could have had it, if only they had dealt effectively with the devil, who came to them in the form of a serpent.

Genesis 3:1-13 tells us:

Now the serpent was more cunning than any beast of the field which the LORD God had made. And he said to the woman, "Has God indeed said, 'You shall not eat of every tree of the garden'?"

And the woman said to the serpent, "We may eat the fruit of the trees of the garden; but of the fruit of the tree which is in the midst of the garden, God has said, 'You shall not eat it, nor shall you touch it, lest you die.'"

Then the serpent said to the woman, "You will not surely die. For God knows that in the day you eat of it your eyes will be opened, and you will be like God, knowing good and evil."

So when the woman saw that the tree was good for food, that it was pleasant to the eyes, and a tree desirable to make one wise, she took of its fruit and ate. She also gave to her husband with her, and he ate. Then the eyes of both of them were opened, and they knew that they were naked; and they sewed fig leaves together and made themselves coverings.

And they heard the sound of the LORD God walking in the garden in the cool of the day, and Adam and his wife hid themselves from the presence of the LORD God among the trees of the garden. Then the LORD God called to Adam and said to him, "Where are you?"

So he said, "I heard Your voice in the garden, and I was afraid because I was naked; and I hid myself."

And He said, "Who told you that you were naked? Have you eaten from the tree of which I commanded you that you should not eat?"

Then the man said, "The woman whom You gave to be with me, she gave me of the tree, and I ate."

And the LORD God said to the woman, "What is this you have done?" The woman said, "The serpent deceived me, and I ate."

Adam and Eve were not just put in a garden; they were put in a *paradise*—a place where every need was met and where they were to grow and enjoy marriage together without end. Even when God had to put them out of the Garden, He never changed His desire and plan for marriage—that it be restored to the paradise He originally intended.

In our culture today that's a little hard to believe. I'm sure that for many people, the greatest pain in their lives has been caused by marriage. That's exactly what the devil wants to do—he wants to take everything God has created for blessing and pleasure and distort it into a source of heartache.

What we see around us today is the fruit of Satan executing that strategy of distortion and perversion concerning sex. The sexual intimacy of a husband and wife is a wonderful, beautiful thing created by God. But Satan takes extra joy in desecrating it, destroying it, and now using it literally to kill people all over the world through the AIDS epidemic and other sexually transmitted diseases.

Nevertheless, marriage is something that God created for good. But there was an enemy, a serpent, in the garden.

BORN INTO A WORLD AT WAR

The reality of what we're dealing with is sobering. Whether we like it or not, we are born into a world at war. Adam and Eve were created in a wonderful paradise. But there was a war going on before their paradise was formed and before they were created. They were born into a world in conflict.

Maybe you're thinking, *Well if there was a war going on, why didn't God warn them?* God did warn them. When He created Adam and Eve, He spoke a blessing over them and instructed them, "Be fruitful and multiply; fill the earth and subdue it; have dominion over the fish of the sea, over the birds of the air, and over every living thing that moves on the earth." The word "rule" is a violent word in the Hebrew language; it means to subjugate by force. It means, "You are going to have to use force to do what I'm telling you to do. There is a battle going on here."

Adam and Eve were warned, but they were extremely naïve and disobedient. What He was telling them was, "You are going to have resistance."

We need to understand that we were born into a world at war—a theater of conflict with marriage at the center—and there is nothing we can do about it. We can't escape it. There are really only two options. We can fight, and win; or we can neglect to fight, and lose.

Can you succeed in marriage? Absolutely! You can have paradise in your marriage, *if* you are willing to fight for it.

Naturally, to be told that we're being sent to the battle front is not what any of us want to hear. That truism reminds me that when I was a young adult, I was very non-political. When I would hear of people voting, campaigning, lobbying or generally getting involved in the political process, I would think, *Not me, man. I am not a political person. I couldn't care less about that stuff.* But through a series of events, I became very aware of the need to be involved in the political arena. I began to understand that in a democracy or republic, political involvement is not only a right, but it is also an obligation for God's people.

Another subject that turned me off as a young man was talk about the devil and spiritual warfare. The topic made me really uncomfortable. When people would talk about the devil doing something, I thought, *You know, I just don't think all of that is the devil. I think you've got this thing all hyped up in your head. I think you're seeing a demon behind every bush. And, frankly, I think you need to grow up and accept the reality of life and be mature about this thing.*

I don't think that way anymore. Today, though I try not to give the devil more credit than he's due, I understand that we have a vicious adversary who is active in every arena of life. You may not believe in the devil, but he certainly believes in you, and he's out to destroy everything that is good in your life.

THE ATTACK IS ON MARRIAGE

The realization that I am in a real war with a real enemy came at the precise point in time when Karen and I came closest to divorce. We were attending a small discipleship group in the church. At the time, we were rank-and-file members. And though our marriage was in the early stages of being healed, we were still dealing with serious issues and fighting a lot. We had been engaged in a running argument about something—I couldn't even tell you what—for about two weeks. That week, when it came time for the Bible study, I told Karen I was staying at home. I was letting her know that wherever she was going that night, I was making it a point to go another direction.

But when Karen came home from that meeting, she uttered some words that would turn our marriage, and our very lives, around.

"I need to tell you what Sarah told me," Karen said as she walked in the door. Sarah and her husband were the leaders of the Bible study.

"What?"

"As soon as I walked inside the house, Sarah said, 'Karen I have to tell you something. I've been praying for you and Jimmy. As I prayed, the Lord gave me a vision of a lion's head in your living room, roaring. It was the devil trying to split you and Jimmy up.'"

The instant Karen repeated that vision, I knew in my heart that it was the truth. The devil had been camped in our home for two weeks trying to break us up. When we started going to that church, I didn't know that I would be its pastor one day, but the devil knew that while pastoring that church a marriage ministry would be born that would impact thousands upon thousands—perhaps millions—of lives.

There was a lot at stake. So he had a tremendous interest in breaking up Jimmy and Karen Evans!

Of course, our enemy has a great interest in breaking up every marriage. We have a mortal enemy who didn't just attack a man and a woman in the Garden of Eden—he attacked marriage itself there.

IT'S WORTH FIGHTING FOR

For a number of reasons, secondary to Jesus Himself, marriage is Satan's ultimate enemy. First Peter 5:8 tells us, "Be sober, be vigilant; because your adversary the devil walks about like a roaring lion, seeking whom he may devour." As I once did, you may think you don't want to have anything to do with that spiritual warfare stuff. But you have no choice in this. You do have something to do with spiritual warfare, because you have an adversary who is trying to kill you. You can tuck tail and run, but if you do, you'll live the rest of your life defeated. Or you can stand up and fight, and live in paradise for the rest of your life.

When Karen came home and told me about that vision of the lion's head, for perhaps the first time in our married lives, we joined hands and took authority over the devil in our marriage and in our home. Instantly, as if you had sprayed air freshener and placed roses all over the house, the whole aroma changed. The atmosphere in our home changed. We stopped fighting and started relating the way we should.

What had finally grabbed our attention was the reality of an invisible presence in our home with an agenda to destroy us. We weren't each other's enemy—Satan was.

From that day to this, when Karen and I wake and pray together, we take authority over certain spiritual elements that we understand are out there. We don't fear the devil; we reverence God and take authority over an enemy already defeated at the Cross. We just actively enforce that defeat. Today we live in a marriage that is blessed because we have fought for that marriage.

You will not have the marriage that God wants you to have unless you are willing to stand and fight for it, because you were born into a world at war, and marriage is Satan's special enemy. Why? Read on and I'll show you.

CHAPTER 18

Satan's Great Terror

There are several important reasons why Satan focuses an inordinate amount of his hellish hatred on the covenant of marriage.

The most significant reason is that marriage is the visible image of Christ's relationship with the Church in this world (see Eph. 5:22-33). In a similar way, marriage projects the very image of God on Earth.

I'm convinced that this is what the Bible teaches us. When Satan sees an individual man or woman, he sees an expression of part of God's nature; but the nature of God is fully represented only in marriage.[1]

"Let *Us* make man in *Our* image," God said (Gen. 1:26, emphasis added). "Let *Us*," not "Let *Me*." This is the Father, the Son and the Holy Spirit speaking within themselves—one God in three persons—saying, "according to Our likeness; let them have dominion." This talk is about warfare and victory: "Dominion over the fish of the sea, over the birds of the air, and over the cattle, over all the earth and over every creeping thing that creeps on the earth. So God created man in His own image; in the image of God He created him; male and female He created them" (vv. 26-27).

How could a God who is three persons in one make someone in His image who isn't plural? God the Father, God the Son and God the Holy Spirit—three persons in one. Three yet one. It's a mystery and a paradox.

Likewise, marriage, the union of both male and female, reflects the image of God.

But, Pastor, God is three, and marriage is only two, you may be thinking.

No, think about it: Marriage is three—man, woman and God—fused together in a mysterious, paradoxical union.

We can break this down even further. God is Father, Son and Holy Spirit. Marriage, then, first of all, is composed of God. Second, it is composed of a man who is commanded to be a Christlike man (see Eph. 5:25-27). Third, it is composed of a woman who is given the same title in the Bible as the Holy Spirit; she is the helper (see Gen. 2:18; John 14:18,26). (Women shouldn't feel demeaned by being called a helpmate; that's exactly what the Holy Spirit is called.)

Jesus said, "When the Helper comes, whom I shall send to you from the Father, the Sprit of truth who proceeds from the Father, he will testify of Me" (John 14:18). So God is God the Father, God the Son and God the Holy Spirit; and marriage is God the Father, a man like Jesus and a woman like the Holy Spirit. Marriage is the image of God. Now we can understand why a righteous marriage absolutely terrifies Satan.

AN IMAGE OF AUTHORITY

An image is very important in what it represents. One of the very first things the United States and the coalition forces did after they defeated Saddam Hussein's regime in Iraq was to tear down his image all over Iraq. Saddam Hussein put up statues and pictures of himself so that everyone would recognize who was boss there. We erased those same images because each was a symbolic projection of his authority. Similar action has been taken by victorious forces throughout the history of war.

In the same way, Satan is trying to take over our cities, our nation and our world. But to do it, he must erase the image of God—which can be found in the institution of marriage. He's trying to tear apart marriages so that God's authority on Earth will be compromised. God said, "Let Us make man in Our image." Satan didn't attack Adam and Eve; he attacked their marriage. And he's been attacking marriages ever since.

It's vital that you understand that Satan is against your marriage. He doesn't want your marriage to succeed. That's why you'll never live in paradise until you stand up and fight him for it.

The image of God is both compound-unity and harmonious-interdependence. God the Father, God the Son and God the Holy Spirit all live for each other. The Father lives for the Son: "This is My beloved Son, in whom I am well pleased" (Matt. 3:17). The Son lives for the Father: "I have glorified [the Father] on the earth. I have finished the work which [He] called Me to do" (John 14:4). And the Spirit of God lives for the Father and the Son to glorify them and to spread their glory all over the earth. Three persons, living completely as one, glorifying each other and living for the other—that's the Trinity, and that's what marriage should reflect.

Two selfless people in a marriage, or groups of people in a church—all living to bless the others selflessly—that's also the image of God. That's what Satan wants to wipe out.

The image of the devil is the opposite of God's image. The image of the devil is singular existence that is self-focused and consumption-minded. It's not three in one, it's one for one. It's runaway individualism. That's why Jesus turned to Peter and said, "Get behind Me, Satan" (Mark 8:33). Peter's mind was set solely on himself.

Whenever you go into a community and see righteous marriages, and people living for family and community, you see a reflection of the image of God. But when you see a bunch of consumption-minded, predatory people living for their own pleasure and using others to get it, that's Satan's agenda. He is trying to obliterate God's image, which is marriage, and set up his own image, which is a horde of selfish people preying on one another for their own personal gratification.

That's why it's up to the Church to rise up and understand that this is a winner-takes-all battle with marriage as the price. In this fight for the very existence of our society, as goes marriage, so goes the rest of society.

ATTACKING THE FOUNDATION

There's another reason Satan has the marriage relationship in his crosshairs. As the first institution God created, marriage is at the foundation of every other social institution that is based on covenant and faithfulness. God created marriage before He created the Church. It predates governments as well as educational and financial institutions. Covenants and agreements are the foundation for everything else in society—marriage being the most important building block for the rest of it.

Satan is a strategist. He understands that his primary attack does not have to be the schools or the government. If he can destroy marriage, then every other institution will fall. That's why we're spending more money per child on education in America than ever before, yet students are learning at the lowest levels in history. It's not primarily because of the system, but because these children are going to school brokenhearted. More children are going through more hell and heartache and going to school in a much worse state of mind than the generation who watched *Leave It to Beaver* and *Father Knows Best*.

Karen and I went to school with intact nuclear families. The worst problem we had was somebody throwing paper wads or calling us names. Children today live in a completely different world.

Satan's ravages do not stop with the destruction of the marriage relationship. One of the leading causes of poverty in America is the breakdown of the family.[2] Satan's strategy: "If I can keep you from a happy marriage, I can destroy everything else that has the potential to bless mankind. Why attack the schools, why attack the financial institutions, why attack the government? All I've got to do is attack marriage; it is the foundation. I don't have to tear down all these walls. I just need to destroy the foundation, and the walls will fall." Thus, Satan is constantly attacking the foundation of our society.

I believe that divorce is the Goliath in our society. God has a tremendous amount of mercy to extend to people who have failed or who are failing in marriage as a result of the mission of the devil to destroy it. But Goliath must be stopped. We must reverse the ignorance of people in general in this arena of warfare. And we can do it with healthy marriages. The biblical story goes that Goliath, who was nine feet tall, stood before the troops of Israel and taunted them until David ran down and killed him. When Goliath fell, every other Philistine warrior fled!

As with David and Goliath, if we can defeat a spirit of divorce in America, we will see poverty flee, our churches become stronger, our school system repair itself and our government corrected. Everything else in society will be fixed once we stop the spirit of divorce and repair the institution of marriage. And the spirit of divorce must be defeated one marriage at a time.

To succeed, we must see that this is not just another battle; it is the main front. It's not a casual conflict; it's a life-and-death struggle. It's not a matter of Satan's having 20 items on his hate list, with number 20 being marriage. Marriage is enemy number 1, except for Satan's hatred of God Himself. When Satan attacks marriage, he is attacking God, the very image of God and the essence of God in our society.

SATAN'S WORST ENEMY

Here's the final reason Satan is terrified of marriage: Marriage will ultimately defeat him.

In the book of Revelation (19:9), we read about the marriage supper of the Lamb. In this amazing passage, we see that the Church is betrothed to Christ, the Lamb. In other words, *we* are the Bride of Christ. In verse 10, Jesus mounts His horse, and we, His Bride, go with Him on the clouds and come down to the final battle with our enemy.

You see, it isn't Jesus alone who defeats Satan, but the army of God, with our husband, Jesus, who defeats him. Marriage defeats him! Immediately following the marriage supper of the Lamb, all of us come through the clouds with our husband and defeat our mortal enemy forever. We are the armies of heaven with Jesus. Satan understands something that we don't—marriage has a special role in the heavenlies. There's a battle going on, and this battle, since the events recorded in Genesis 3, has infused the subject of marriage on Earth.

I hope you now have a better appreciation for how important marriage is to God. The hurt, the strife and the abuse that are so much a part of marriage for many people are not His plan or His doing. If your marriage is currently a source of pain, it's not because God doesn't want to give you a paradise. He wants to bless you with a marriage that will last for the rest of your life, meet your needs and be a place of abundance and pleasure for you. But the reality is that you will have to deal with the serpent to experience paradise in marriage.

Karen and I almost lost it all because I was so completely unaware of the devil's presence and his designs on our marriage. Once we, by the grace of God, became aware of what the devil was doing, and we began to take authority over him, everything changed.

It is with good reason that God said in Genesis 2:18, "It is not good that man should be alone." There are some things in your life that God cannot do without marriage. (Yes, some believers have a special calling to be single, but they are a minority—perhaps 6 to 7 percent of the population. If you know that you are called to be single, you are still called to a marriage. You've got to be married to Jesus to reach your full potential and get where God is taking you. Single people are not called to be a sub-culture; they are called to be a super-culture. They are elite forces in the army of God, but they are a minority.)

The vast majority of men and women desire to be married and should be married. In fact, in one survey conducted in Washington State more than 90 percent of the people surveyed said that they greatly desire a stable marriage for a lifetime.[3]

God is saying, *I want you to be married. It's not just your desire, but it's my desire for you too.*

God looked at Adam and said, "It is not good. I can't fulfill the purpose I want to fulfill in Adam as long as he's by himself. He's incomplete. I'm going to make a helper for Adam so that I can fulfill the destiny that I want to fulfill for him."

The marriage relationship is a huge issue. It's a primary issue. We must do everything we can to develop and nurture our marriages.

Notes

1. A Note to Christian Singles: Occasionally, when I teach this truth, I hear from a single person who is offended or disappointed that I might suggest they are not a full expression of God's image. There is certainly a small minority of believers who are called by God to singleness and celibacy. These are a very special group (they're not a subculture in the Body of Christ, they're a super-culture!). For them, as Paul implies in 1 Corinthians 7, God is their portion. He personally completes the picture for them. Nevertheless, the passage in Ephesians 6 makes it clear that there is a "great mystery" involved in the way a man and a woman become "one flesh" in marriage. And this mysterious joining together represents something very spiritually powerful—something the enemy thoroughly detests and greatly fears.

2. Patrick F. Fagan, Robert E. Rector, Kirk A. Johnson, Ph.D., and America Peterson, *The Positive Effects of Marriage: A Book of Charts* (Washington, D.C.: The Heritage Foundation, 2002), n.p.

3. "Families Northwest Releases 'The State of Our Unions' Marriage Survey Report," *Families Northwest,* February 7, 2005. http://www.familiesnorthwest.org/fnw.aspx ?pid=212 (accessed February 2006).

CHAPTER 19

The Serpent Busters

Here is what we've learned in this section thus far: Marriage is vital. God meant it to be a paradise. Satan hates it.

Those facts prompt the question, How are we going to succeed in ridding the garden of our marriage of its mortal enemy? Three standards characterize a serpent-free paradise—standards that will help you understand why (if you have a divorce in your past) the devil was successful in destroying your marriage.

The first standard is acceptance of God's Word as the final authority in your life, in your marriage and in your decision-making. The first words the devil said to mankind when he appeared to them were, "Has God really said . . . ?"

We are told that the Bible is the Sword of the Spirit, and with it we can vanquish the enemy. In other words, he cannot defeat us until he disarms us. So, the first thing the devil did when he came into the Garden of Eden was attack the integrity of the Word of God.

You are probably aware of how aggressively the integrity of the Word of God is being attacked in America today. Studies by The Barna Group, a Christian research organization, revealed that only 40 percent of born-again Christians in America consult the Bible when they are making important moral or ethical decisions.[1] Shockingly, Barna also reported that the divorce rate is slightly *higher* among Christians than among non-Christians. The appalling truth is that if you are a non-Christian in America, you statistically have a slightly better chance of succeeding in marriage than you do if you are a Christian! That is an abomination to God and shows that marriage is failing in America to the precise extent the Word of God has been rejected as the basis of authority.

Recently, the Anglican Church of Canada, a member of the Anglican Communion of the Episcopalian Church, affirmed the "integrity and sanctity" of same-sex marriages. This is a slap to the face of God and His Word. Christian leaders who call themselves pastors or teachers and yet refuse to acknowledge the authority of God's Word would be more honest to throw the Bible away, get a newspaper or a college sociology textbook and call that their authoritative reference.

The Bible is God's revealed Word to us. Second Timothy 3:16 tells us, "All Scripture is given by inspiration of God, and is profitable for doctrine, for reproof, for correction, for instruction in righteousness." Jesus said, "It is written, 'Man shall not live by bread alone, but by every word that proceeds from the mouth of God' " (Matt. 4:4).

To succeed in marriage, you must decide how you are going to make your decisions. On what authority do you base your life? By what star do you navigate? What compass determines true North for you?

In the Barna study, when Christians were asked how they made their decisions, the vast majority said they based decisions on what they thought would bring the best result (rather than by what the Word of God plainly declares).[2] This is catastrophic.

I can promise you by the authority of the Word of God, and by the positive results of decades of living based upon it, that the Word works. It always brings the best results! Satan cannot defeat you while you are armed with and guided by the Word of God.

One of Satan's tactics is to try to make us feel embarrassed about believing the Word of God. I do not feel the least bit embarrassed about believing that God's Word is true and reliable. It has saved my life. It *is* my life.

Jesus said, "Man shall not live by bread alone, but by every word that proceeds from the mouth of God." This—by what God's Word says—is how you live. Jesus said, "The words that I speak to you are spirit, and they are life" (John 6:63).

ADAM AND EVE'S TWO COMMANDS

God gave Adam and Eve two commandments. In essence, their Bible had only two verses. One was a command to do something; the other was a command to avoid something.

In similar fashion, a person can only commit two types of sin. The first is a sin of *commission*: "I'm choosing to do something God told me *not* to do." The other is the sin of *omission*: "I am choosing not to do something God told me to do."

The positive command given to Adam and Eve was to "be fruitful and multiply; fill the earth and subdue it; have dominion over the fish of the sea, over the birds of the air, and over every living thing that moves on the earth" (Gen. 1:28). The negative command was, "Of every tree of the garden you may freely eat; but of the tree of the knowledge of good and evil you shall not eat, for in the day that you eat of it you shall surely die" (Gen. 2:16-17).

Before Adam and Eve ever ate of the fruit of the forbidden tree (a sin of commission), they had already committed sins of omission. I believe that when the devil showed up in the Garden of Eden to tempt Adam and Eve, they did not have a child. Yet they had been commanded to be fruitful and multiply, to fill the earth and subdue it. We know that when the devil came in and began to accuse God, Adam didn't stand up and subdue him. He did not take dominion over every creeping thing the way God had commanded him. Though Adam and Eve could have freely eaten of the tree in the middle of the garden that would have let them live forever, they had never eaten of that tree. We know this because as soon as they had sinned, God chased them out of the Garden of Eden so they could not go and eat of the tree of life.

I would think that the first thing Adam and Eve would have done would be to eat of the tree of life, as God had instructed. But they were apathetic toward the Word of God. The reason Satan could defeat them is that they hadn't done the things God had told them to do.

I'm convinced that God would not have allowed them to be tested if they hadn't had time to do the right thing concerning having children. The number-one thing God wanted to do through Adam and Eve was to extend His kingdom in all the world through physical multiplication: "Be fruitful and multiply."

So how long did God wait from the time He created them until the time He allowed the devil to tempt them? The Bible doesn't tell us, but my opinion is that God waited long enough for Eve to conceive. It takes nine months to have a baby, but only hours to conceive. In other words, it wouldn't have taken them long to be obedient to what God said.

Look again at the second command God gave: "Of every tree of the garden you may freely eat; but of the tree of the knowledge of good and evil you shall not eat, for in the day that you eat of it you shall surely die" (Gen. 2:16-17). God gave this command before He created Eve; so it was Adam's responsibility to accurately teach it to her. But he didn't, because when Eve was tempted by the devil, she couldn't accurately recite the commandment back to him.

Adam didn't take seriously his responsibility as the priest of the home. We already know that he was apathetic, because he didn't rise up and kill the serpent when it came and began to deceive his wife. And he had not properly communicated the Word of God to his wife.

All of this paints a picture of Adam and Eve failing to take the Word of God to heart. Before they committed that fatal sin of commission, they had already established a pattern of sins of omission. They had little regard for the Word of the Lord. And without the Word to guard their thoughts and actions, they were no match for the devil's deception and manipulation. The first thing the enemy said was, "Has God really said . . . ?" In other words, "Surely God didn't mean what He said!"

Do you see the devil's strategy? And today we realize that he has done a very effective job of taking the Bible and making it into something we are ashamed of. People are ashamed of the Word of God, ashamed of the unfashionable standards of the Bible, ashamed of the Holy Spirit and His gifts and ashamed of the Word's clear and unequivocal proclamation that Jesus is the only way to heaven.

To have a serpent-free paradise, we must decide that we will not be ashamed of God's Word. It is "the power of God to salvation for everyone who believes" (Rom. 1:16). Then why would we be ashamed of it?

Hebrews 4:12 says, "The word of God is living and powerful, and sharper than any two-edged sword . . . and is a discerner of the thoughts and intents of the heart."

You read every other book in the world. But this book reads you!

That's what Satan fears. The Bible is the Sword of the Spirit in the cosmic battle taking place in the heavenlies (see Eph. 6:17). Scripture was the weapon Jesus relied on when He was attacked by Satan in the wilderness. Jesus vanquished the devil by saying, "It is written" over and over again (see Matt. 4:4-7). Jesus quoted three scriptures, and the devil fled. So who do we think we are? How do we think we're going to win this battle of life—this struggle for our marriages and our families—without the resource that was vital to our Lord's victory over the enemy? Knowledge of God's Word is the only way we are going to succeed.

When Karen and I were raising our children, the media and institutions were filled with a lot of politically correct nonsense about parenting and discipline. But I didn't care what the so-called experts were saying. What I cared about was living my life in the right way before God and doing things His way. I knew that I would only get one chance at this parenting thing, and I was determined to do it by the Book.

That is the only way to live your life. If you want to be happily married but you don't believe this, you have precious little chance of succeeding. But if you want to be married and you are willing to do it this way, you have a 100 percent chance of success. God's Word is the standard. It is the weapon that will defeat the devil and keep him away.

PARTNERSHIP: A POWERFUL WEAPON

The second standard of a serpent-free paradise is partnership—true accountability to each other under God's authority in your lives.

Genesis 3:4 tells us, "The serpent said to the woman . . ." Satan always divides before he conquers. Karen and I have a simple understanding in our marriage: We will not make any significant decision without the other person involved. We don't buy or do anything of significance on our own. I do not make decisions related to my ministry or my job without Karen's full knowledge and support. Everything has been done with her full awareness, and she acts in the same way.

Jesus said, "[A] house divided against itself will not stand" (Matt. 12:25). That's why the devil divides couples. That's the way he came against Adam and Eve, not coming to them when they were together as a couple, but separating Eve from Adam, he attacked her in her position of vulnerability. We were never designed to fight and win on our own. Jesus said, "If two of you agree on earth concerning anything that they ask, it will be done for them by My Father in heaven" (Matt. 18:19). The reason He didn't say, "If one person agrees, it will be done" is because Jesus will not honor an independent spirit. Every time Jesus sent a disciple out to minister, He sent the person out with someone else, two by two. Jesus understands the power of partnership.

Likewise, the devil understands the power of isolation. Our greatest fear is of being alone. It's why we're so afraid of being rejected and being unpopular. It's why we're so afraid of what people think and what they do concerning us.

In marriage and in the Body of Christ, God has created a system in which we never have to be alone. But being together means being accountable. It comes with the territory. That's why the seedbed of all sin is *independence* and the seedbed of all righteousness is *interdependence*—upon God and upon each other.

Hebrews 10:24-25 tells us, "Let us consider one another in order to stir up love and good works, not forsaking the assembling of ourselves together, as is the manner of some, but exhorting one another, and so much the more as you see the Day approaching." We may be living in the final moments before the coming of Jesus Christ. As you see that day approaching, do not isolate yourself the way that some people do; rather, come together all the more. Why? Because as the world becomes increasingly full of a spirit of lawlessness, we will need each other more. We must have connection—relationship.

The enemy is using some elements in our modern society to undermine the spirit of partnership. In the American psyche, there is a strong streak of personal independence that can work against us. Instead of seeing our freedom as the right to choose to whom we will give honor, service and accountability, we've taken it to mean that we don't have to be accountable to anybody.

The libertarian or libertine spirit of the age seems to promote, "Nobody is going to tell me what to do."

Japan is in a crisis over this same spirit. That nation (like much of Europe) has begun to experience negative population growth. Old folks are dying at a faster rate than they are being replaced. Increasing numbers of their young people are choosing not to marry. They have convinced themselves to live their lives purely for themselves—isolated and alone. The rate of marriage and births is so low that the government is trying to find ways to talk their young people into having sex and having babies. Self-centered, self-serving isolation is precisely what the devil is after.

If Satan has his way, we will ultimately be living by ourselves, cut off and alone in little media cocoons with iPod earphones in our ears, using our mobile phones to send text messages to friends we never actually see.

No one will want to be married. And no one will want to go to church, because nobody wants to get hurt. This is one of the defining characteristics of the last days: "Because lawlessness will abound, the love of many will grow cold" (Matt. 24:12).

God says, "Therefore a man shall leave his father and mother and be joined to his wife, and they shall become one flesh" (Gen. 2:24). Thus, a successful marriage requires agreement between husband and wife that in their marriage, they will be absolutely one. Each spouse agrees that he or she will not make a decision without the other. They pray together about everything that goes on in their home. They are united. They are one.

When Satan tries to divide such a couple, it's like trying to divide God Himself. Satan can't do that. But when Satan comes to a man and a woman who don't talk, who don't pray together, who are living separate lives under the same roof, he just blows on their relationship and it shatters. There is nothing to it.

A spirit of independence and isolation is what left Adam and Eve's relationship vulnerable. Rather than making Adam or God a part of her decision, Eve made a decision on her own. It cost her a life in paradise.

TAKE YOUR RIGHTFUL PLACE

A third standard for a serpent-free paradise is the need to consistently take authority over Satan in the realm of the spirit. Jesus said, "I give you the authority to trample on serpents and scorpions, and over all the power of the enemy, and nothing shall by any means hurt you" (Luke 10:19). And in Matthew 18:18-20, He promised that "whatever you bind on earth will be bound in heaven, and whatever you loose on earth will be loosed in heaven. Again I say to you that if two of you agree on earth concerning anything that they ask, it will be done for them by My Father in heaven. For where two or three are gathered together in My name, I am there in the midst of them."

God has given us full authority in the realm of the spirit over all the power of the devil. When Karen and I pray for our marriage, we join hands and declare things in this way: "In the name of Jesus, we bind a spirit of rebellion over our children. We take authority over this, and this and this . . ." Whatever Karen and I are facing, we don't worry about it; we pray about it. We pray over everything. Looking back over 27 years of doing that, I can say with confidence that it absolutely works. Jesus said "nothing shall by any means harm you" because of the authority he has given us (see Luke 10:19).

Why then are so many of God's people devastated? It's because they don't step into the authority that is theirs through prayer. Jesus said, "*Nothing* shall by any means harm you." So why is America so devastated? It's because we don't believe Jesus' promise. In fact, we are ashamed of it. We are ashamed of looking like fanatics when we pray. We are ashamed of showing that we believe the real battle is in the invisible realm.

It's easier (and much more socially acceptable) to think the problem is your spouse or some behavioral problem in your children. Sometimes there will be problems in those areas, but the root problem is never flesh and blood, it is in the unseen realm of the spirit.

A man I have known for a long time, a very stable believer, approached me in church one day and told me something I had never heard him talk about before.

"Pastor Jimmy, I saw demons around my house the other day. I was driving into my driveway after work, and I saw demons around my house. I have never before seen anything like it. But when I saw those evil spirits, the Lord told me, 'Begin to pray for your children.'

"For two weeks, I prayed for my children. In that two-week period, my son almost died twice: He was almost killed in a car wreck, and then he was hospitalized and almost died from a seizure that is still unexplained. I believe the devil was trying to kill my son, and God warned me to pray for him."

This was extraordinary language for this gentleman. This is not a man who sees the devil behind every bush. This is a godly man whom God graced with a brief opening of his eyes to the realm of the spirit in order to expose the devil's stalking of his family. I believe his son is alive today because this man acted on what God had shown him and told him.

Please know that you don't have to be afraid of the devil. God is so much more powerful than Satan: "He who is in you is greater than he who is in the world" (1 John 4:4). But also know that you have an enemy you can beat only if you are willing to fight. If you don't, you'll lose. He is out to kill you. If you understood how evil the devil is, if you understood the schemes he has to wreak havoc in your life, you would go home, take the hand of your spouse and pray to bind him. You would wake up every morning with your Sword on, ready to fight. And you would never let him win.

First John 3:8 says that the purpose for which Jesus came was to destroy the works of the devil. Jesus came on a military mission to destroy the devil and everything he was doing. And by His Spirit and His Word, He left you the authority of God in your home and in your marriage and in your family to live in an absolute paradise, if you are willing to fight for it.

It's no mystery. If you don't pray, if you don't believe, if you choose to believe what the television is saying rather than what God is saying, you are dead. You and your family are already defeated. It will be hard to succeed. Your family will be in ultimate misery. You may be popular, but you are going to be miserable.

To win, you must understand that there's a battle going on in the unseen realm and you must be sober and vigilant about your part in that battle.

FROM TARGET TO VICTOR

The devil's war is not against you as an individual. The true focus of his hate is your marriage. He doesn't care a bit about you. He doesn't give a rip about the rest of your life or your eternity. He doesn't care about you at all. He cares that every single time you and your spouse get together and start loving each other selflessly, you bear the image of God to your children and to all of society. And like an enemy trying to conquer another king's territory, he's trying to rip down the image of his adversary, God.

He comes through our communities and our nation trying to devour and destroy us. But every time he sees a happy couple, it enrages him because he sees the image of his archenemy. He cannot tolerate it, because it's an extension of the authority of God.

At some point, we the people of God must say that we're tired of being the ones who don't believe the Bible, and the ones who divorce the most. We should be the ones who stay married the longest! We should be the ones who understand the reality of what is going on all around us.

Back when Karen and I were fighting, and I told her that she could go to that Bible study alone, I did not want to be where she was. I thought she was the problem in our marriage. But there was a lion in our home that was roaring and trying to drive us apart—an enemy who understood that we had a destiny. He understood that we were going to harm him; we were going to affect his kingdom. And we have.

That enemy knows the same thing about you. If he can keep you isolated—if he can keep you hurting, selfish and miserable—he knows that you will be no threat to him. But once you are married according to God's design, once you love the way that God wants you to love, you can destroy him. So he looks for every opportunity to strike preemptively. He doesn't wait until you are anointed and standing on a platform. The moment you get married, you are on the platform, and the war begins.

Today, Karen and I live in peace. We live in abundance. We live in love. We live in a wonderful home with a wonderful family—not a family without problems, but a family that lives very closely to the way God ordained us to live. Our family prays all the time and takes authority in the realm of the spirit all the time. That's our lifestyle.

From reading God's Word and from our personal experience, I can tell you that you can succeed if you will do what we have done. Even if you've been divorced nine times, God loves you and has a plan for your success. He doesn't throw people away. He doesn't give up on people.

You may have made every mistake you can imagine, but He forgives every mistake. Where sin abounds, grace abounds so much more (see Rom. 5:20). Many of us, in making the mistakes we have made, just haven't understood what's been going on all around us. We haven't accurately perceived reality. But once we do understand the true nature of the battle that is being waged against our marriages, we can take the war against marriage seriously, fight for it, and win for the rest of our lives.

We *can* live in a serpent-free paradise.

Notes

1. George Barna, *Think Like Jesus: Make the Right Decision Every Time* (Nashville, TN: Integrity Publishers), 2003, n.p.
2. Ibid.

A Serpent-Free Paradise

We were born into a world at war—a theater of conflict with marriage at its center. There are really only two options. We can fight to save marriage and win, or we can neglect to fight and lose.

Prayer, Partnership and Purpose

*Better is a dry morsel with quietness, than a
house full of feasting with strife.*

Proverbs 17:1

*Oh Thou, who dwellest in so many homes, possess Thyself
of this. Bless the life that is sheltered here. Grant that trust
and peace and comfort abide within, and that love and
life and usefulness may go out from this home forever.*

Traditional Irish House Blessing

CHAPTER 20

A Place of Peace

Is relational paradise possible for you and your mate? What would it look like? Feel like? Sound like? And if it is possible to get to such a place in your relationship, wouldn't you do whatever was necessary to get there?

Let's leave those questions for a moment and think about what would characterize an actual place in order to call it paradise. If you asked a large group of people, I'm sure there would be four fundamental characteristics—or pleasures—common to everyone's perception of paradise. Indeed, there are four aspects that *must* be present for a place to be a true "Eden." Those four characteristics are *visual beauty, abundance, sensual pleasure* and *profound peace.*

1. *Visual beauty.* Yes, it's difficult to imagine a paradise that wouldn't be a delight to the visual senses.
2. *Abundance.* Paradise is simply not a place you associate with lack or with scraping by with the bare necessities for survival. You expect paradise to be a place in which there is plenty to meet your needs, to give away to others, and to invest for even greater return in the future.
3. *Sensual pleasure.* Paradise is a place in which the climate, the water, the fragrance of the air and the comforts all stimulate and affirm the joy of being alive. This is a place that is a delight to the senses.

4. *Profound peace.* Paradise is a place where there is no conflict—a place where you feel safe and can rest in the deepest part of your being. This is a place where you can lower your guard and drop your defenses.

Not only are these four elements common to any natural paradise, but they also should, in certain ways, characterize the secret paradise of marriage.

Now, if you think about it, the first three of those elements—beauty, abundance and pleasure—are not all that uncommon in many marriages, especially in modern-day Western culture. In my opinion, there has never been more access to aesthetic beauty than in America today. Parks, public places, even shopping malls and developments are all designed and built with visual appeal in mind.

On a personal level, most people want to be married to a person they are visually attracted to. This is not abnormal—God made it that way. We pair up based on mutual attraction. And today we have a lot of options to enhance our natural attractiveness.

Likewise, relative abundance is also very accessible. In fact, there has never been as much abundance (not only in our culture but also world-wide) as there is today. And there has never been as much comfort and positive sensual pleasure as we have today in American society. Food is cheap, diverse and widely available (in fact, we're being told that our biggest health crisis in this nation stems from having too much to eat!). We don't work from dawn to dusk seven days a week as people did just a few generations back—dragging home at night with just enough energy to get to bed.

We live and work in comfortable, climate-controlled environments and are surrounded by an array of opportunities with which to be entertained. If we choose to use it, we have ample leisure time to give attention to and spend quality time with one another.

I've counseled hundreds of couples who possessed the first three elements of paradise—*beauty, plenty of money* and *sensual pleasure*—yet they didn't have the marriage they were looking for. Their marriages were crying out for the vital fourth ingredient of paradise—the element of *peace*.

There is a tremendous hunger to experience peace in the marriage relationship. And it's a primary expectation for people who are entering a marriage. That expectation is understandable, because without peace, all the other ground we gain in improving our relationships can rapidly erode. The healing, the passion, the friendship, the sexual intimacy—everything is at risk if we don't find the answer to living peacefully with one another.

Peace in marriage is not an impossible dream. Far from it! By establishing four simple foundations, a husband and wife can open wide the door to peace and slam shut the door to strife in their marriage.

THE FIRST FOUNDATION: PRIOR AGREEMENT

Amos 3:3 says, "Can two walk together unless they are agreed?" In more modern phraseology: Without first agreeing on some basic things about the trip, how can two people make any progress together? It's a rhetorical question. The obvious answer is, They can't. Two people who are not in agreement simply cannot journey together—not peacefully anyway. Their journey will be a constant battle: *What's our destination? We should turn left here! We need to go faster!* The fact is, unless you're in agreement before the journey begins, you're not going to make much forward progress, and the progress you do make will be painful.

This is especially true of the longest two-person journey in life— marriage.

I discovered many years ago, in my very first assignment in ministry—pre-marriage counseling—that very few couples have been even remotely prepared for their journey together. They have not talked enough to identify and agree on how they will respond to the significant issues every husband and wife face. More than 95 percent of the couples who have come to my office in preparation for marriage haven't had a deep conversation about anything in the marriage relationship beyond where to go on the honeymoon and what china pattern to register.

Sure, they have had brief, superficial conversations, but no significant dialogue about values, goals or boundaries.

In my counseling sessions, I had couples discuss some serious things. I led them to talk through the real issues they would face in the relationship—to compare their assumptions about where they were headed and what was important. And when I did, one out of five couples decided not to get married.

Think about that for a moment.

After being forced to discuss some very fundamental issues that would eventually confront them on their journey together, they came to an impasse. They discovered they were incompatible, unable to come to agreement on one or more major decisions they would soon face in their lives together.

Let me give you an example of some of the questions I would ask couples to discuss. The first group of questions deals with marriage expectations: *How many children, if any, are you going to have?* When I asked one couple that question, he said "Two." She said, "Six!"

Is the wife going to work? Do you want to guess how many times the woman has said no and the man has said, "Of course she is"?

Here are some other questions about which a couple can have widely different expectations: *Who will manage the money? How much are you going to spend without your spouse's approval? Whose family will you spend the holidays with? How will you deal with in-law problems?*

Another series of questions centers on role concepts: *Who will do the housework? Mow the yard? Discipline the kids? Is it okay for a woman to initiate sex?* When I went through that series of questions with one couple, the young man said, "She'll do the house work. She'll mow the yard. She'll to discipline the kids, and, no, she can't initiate sex." She was flabbergasted. They had never talked about these basic issues in a way that would have revealed his underlying chauvinistic expectations.

It's not only couples who are preparing for marriage that aren't talking. I can't tell you the number of couples who come for counseling five years into their relationship who have never sat down and discussed vital issues. Without those conversations, there is no hope for arriving at prior agreement.

Three Levels of Communication in Marriage

Obviously, prior agreement requires meaningful communication. But not all communication is effective. Communication can take place on at least three different levels—*proactive, reactive* and *radioactive* levels.

Proactive communication is talking about things *before* experiencing them. It's talking about children before you have them. It's discussing how much money you're going to spend and how much money you're going to save *before* you earn it. In other words, it's having a plan for the future and for everything in your life together. To communicate proactively is to position yourselves for a peaceful journey. There will not be a lot of strife and negative emotion when situations arise, because you've already agreed upon what you're going to do.

Without proactive communication, your interaction easily degenerates into *reactive communication*. This communication level inevitably occurs when couples do not talk in-depth, in advance, about key areas of their relationship. Though they are journeying together, they really don't agree. They have agreed to travel, but because they didn't agree about the trip in detail, every turn in their journey sparks a fresh argument: *Are we going to take that turn? Are we not going to take that turn? Are we going to stop here or go forward?*

Tremendous tension arises in the relationship because of the constant reaction to issues. Emotions fray, annoyance mushrooms and things are said that shouldn't be said:

"If you would just be quiet and follow along, we wouldn't have all these problems."

"Oh really? Well, the reason we have all these problems is because every time something happens, you're just so reactive."

These kinds of comments reveal that a couple hasn't yet realized that reaction is inevitable on any issue for which they haven't agreed beforehand. Issues not agreed on ignite reactivity. If the lack of agreement continues, communication on some of those issues can degenerate to the third level of communication.

This third level of communication is what I call *radioactive communication*. This condition arises when couples seemingly cannot talk, resolve issues or agree in any proactive way. In-laws, for example, frequently become a radioactive issue. Money often becomes radioactive as well.

A radioactive issue is one that is consistently damaging to the relationship. It's an issue that is recurring, touchy, explosive and soon labeled off-limits. These issues are identified as part of a radioactive zone. Couples stop addressing them—they learn to steer clear of them lest an argument break out.

Every radioactive issue is one that should have been discussed proactively but was put off or ignored. It became reactive, and finally became radioactive—incendiary, dangerous and off-limits.

Disarming the Radioactive Issues

So how can you diffuse the radioactive issues, reverse the tendency toward reactivity and move into a consistently proactive level of communication in your marriage?

First, clear out the radioactive issues by agreeing together to discuss everything—absolutely *nothing* can remain off limits. In some relationships, radioactive issues may be numerous. Those couples do not need to try to fix things themselves. They need to seek outside help. Karen and I had to do that. More than once, we had to go outside of our marriage to get help because we were responding so emotionally to certain issues. We've taught our children that when they have problems in their marriages that they can't resolve, they should not hesitate to get help. And that's what they do.

Getting help is not a sign of weakness; on the contrary, it's a sign of wisdom. People who succeed in marriage (and in other areas of life) are people with humble, teachable spirits. We all need to embrace this fact of life: If we excel at something, it is because we have a teachable spirit in that area. If we fail repeatedly, it's an indicator that in that area we are unteachable (probably because we're prideful and self-sufficient).

If you're failing in your marriage and you can't settle the conflict between the two of you, get help! Together, tell a Christian counselor, a pastor or someone else who is qualified to help you. Say, "This is our issue. We're submitting this to you. We're asking God to give you wisdom for this situation, and we need your input."

Put that radioactive issue in the light and let God heal it. Don't let the thing stay between you. Don't allow that issue to continue to create headbutting sessions that escalate to the point where it has to be your way or the highway. Discuss it. Be willing to humble yourself and let someone else speak into your life.

How will you know when an issue is no longer radioactive? When you agree on it and you're both at peace. You've made the past the past, forgiven one another and moved on. It's the point at which you both have the same understanding related to that issue.

Not surprisingly, the second step toward proactive communication is to stop all the reacting. And the only way you can do this is to make sure you are communicating proactively about every major issue. This is the only way to remove the issues that create reaction between you.

A big, practical step toward building a lifestyle of proactive communication is to have a vision and to plan a retreat at least once a year. This is a time set aside for discussing everything in your marriage with the goal of total agreement. Karen and I do this faithfully. Not only do we schedule it at least once a year, but we also schedule it any other time when we have identified a new area of disagreement that is threatening to create tension in our marriage. (How can two walk together unless they agree?)

Tension is the danger signal that we don't have the same vision in some area. Proverbs 29:18 tells us, "Where there is no vision, the people are unrestrained" *(NASB)*. You can't keep people going together in the same direction unless they have the same vision. What is your vision for your children? For your finances? For your marriage? For your sex life? What is your vision for your relationship, and how is that vision going to affect other people? What are you trying to accomplish?

The bottom line is this: If you don't have a vision, you can't make decisions that are bigger than what you're already facing. You have no basis to decide what to do and what not to do. Without vision, you can't help but constantly react to issues and be on opposite sides, pulling against each other.

So take three or four days and go away somewhere. In the mornings, when you wake up, pray and talk together. Identify all the areas in which you need to find agreement to get clear vision. In humility, submit to God and to each other to address every one of those areas and get the mind of God on all of them. Commit to discussing them one by one and praying about them.

In the afternoons and evenings, just have fun. Your goal for the end of the retreat is to be in agreement about everything and committed to living true to what you say about money, kids, schedules, in-laws, holidays, and every other issue you pray and agree about. That's called prior agreement. And it creates a peaceful atmosphere for the rest of the year.

Next, support the agreements made during your retreat with regular times of communication about real issues. Communicate about the things that matter. Sit down and talk face-to-face; refuse to let tension build up. If you find yourself reacting to something in the day-to-day course of your relationship, don't shove it aside. Sit down right then and pray about it and discuss it until you come to agreement. Do this when you see a challenging issue or situation coming up. Talk about it in detail until you know that you agree and have the same vision for how you are going to respond.

Prior agreement is one of the things that bring peace into the relationship.

The Second Foundation: Purpose

One of the most popular books in the country over the last few years has been Rick Warren's *The Purpose-Driven Life*. The powerful, jarring first words of Rick's book are, "It's not about you."

That's true, you know. Your life *is* about something bigger than you.

I mention this because the second foundation of peace in a marriage relationship is *purpose*—finding God's purpose for your life together. Purpose is related to what we've already talked about—sharing a vision. But it's bigger than that.

Ask yourselves, Why did God put us together? It's hard to make the smaller decisions when you don't understand the bigger picture. Yet most people can't answer the question, What is God's greater purpose for us as a couple? If you don't find a purpose greater than you, you're going to live your life in chaos and disappointment. If you're living only for yourself, or even for your own family or marriage, your life will constantly be one of disappointment. Why? Because you were created by a great God to do something bigger and beyond you. You've got to find that purpose and live for something bigger than you.

Let me give you an example of some things Karen and I decided were the purpose of our marriage. First, we agreed that we were brought together to raise godly children to serve the Lord and reach the next generation. And we have fulfilled that purpose. Our children are grown, and they are godly people serving the Lord and positively impacting their communities. Malachi 2:13-16 not only tells us that God hates divorce, but it also gives us His reason: He wants righteous offspring. Divorce affects children in a negative way. Our purpose together is to raise righteous kids.

Second, we are to be a witness for God's love to reach other people. A good marriage is the most profound proclamation of the love of Jesus Christ in the world. It is, according to Ephesians 5, a walking portrait of Jesus and the Church. Karen and I desire that our marriage be so profoundly good that people find God just by watching us together. And don't be deceived, people *are* watching. If you don't believe it, just live a happy marriage in front of them and see how many of them come to you for advice.

People are constantly looking at you. That's why it's so important not to live just for yourself. It's why Karen and I don't bicker in public. We want our marriage to be great. People are looking at us, and we want our witness to be something that will have an effect on others for Christ.

Third, we are to use our gifts to serve a local church. Our marriage means that together we're going to give of our finances and of our time to our church. The local church is the hope of the world. So we have purposed to use the grace and wisdom God has given us in the area of family and marriage to help others in need.

Karen and I love giving to others the grace that Jesus gave to us when we were having marriage trouble. Because of what we've been through, we know firsthand what God can do for the many couples who may have picked up this book in the midst of great discouragement about their marriages. We know what He can do for them—what He can do for you.

Right now, you may be thinking that you must have one of the worst marriages imaginable; yet not only does God want to heal your marriage, but He also wants to use you to help other people's marriages once yours is whole. As ridiculous as that might seem right now, it's absolutely true, because people in trouble find it much easier to receive from those who have worked through the problems than from those who never had any challenges in their relationship.

That doesn't mean that a couple has to go through all kinds of relational hell to help others; but to whatever extent they have had to work through issues, they will understand what other couples are going through. If you've been at death's door as far as your marriage was concerned and seen God bring your relationship back to life, as He did for Karen and me, that redeemed marriage can in turn save dozens of other marriages and help other families.

Your good marriage could make the difference in the life of a child whose parents stay together because of you. One of the greatest thoughts I go to bed with each night is the knowledge that my life and work helps keep vulnerable children's moms and dads together. That's a very real effect of our ministry.

I mention it because Karen and I have found that doing something greater than just wondering how our own needs and desires will be met helps us answer the smaller questions. When we're considering what to do with our money or our time, we understand that we are living under a greater purpose. Anything on Earth that doesn't point heavenward is wrong, because everything we have and do is measured against the greater purpose.

You see, there's only one story going on, and that's the story of Jesus Christ. That's the story that begins and ends everything. That's why the Bible says, "In Him we live and move and have our being" (Acts 17:28).

What a horrible thing for 6 billion people to be on the earth at this critical time in history and miss the real story because they think it's all about them!

Life, and whatever you are going through right now, is just too big to be about you. Walk outside tonight, look up in the sky, gaze at the vast expanse of the stars in God's creation and see if it doesn't say something to you. See if it doesn't say that this whole thing is just too big to be about you. It has to be about Him. When we understand that, and we stop living for ourselves and start living for Him, everything begins to work.

Now do you see why it's so vital that you sit down together and talk and pray about things beforehand, believing that God will clearly show you why He put you two together? Some couples who take this important step end up seeing that God has put them together with their abilities for the purpose of making financial resources to bring in to the Church to supply God's kingdom. Others will discover they have a profound ministry together—maybe as leaders in their church. If you seek God's purpose for putting you together as a couple, you will find it—and there will be more than just one purpose.

When you find God's purpose in your marriage, peace comes into your relationship because God comes into your relationship. Jesus told us to "pray this way every day: let Your kingdom come, let Your will be done, here on Earth exactly the way that it's done there in heaven" (see Matt. 6:10-13). When God's rule and purpose comes, His peace comes with it. And it's the most profound thing in the world.

THE THIRD FOUNDATION: PARTNERSHIP

John Gottman of the University of Washington has conducted hundreds of hours of research on marriage and divorce. In one study, he took 130 newly married couples and tracked their relationship for six years. At the end of that period, he followed up with a very detailed study of their relationships. He noted the couples that were happy and those that weren't. Then he identified the most significant common denominator for every happy couple.

It was simply "shared control in the relationship." That's it. Just a sense of shared control![1]

That's why I call the third foundation for peace in marriage, *partnership*. Make sure that you do everything as partners, with neither spouse dominating the other. Everything in marriage has to be an equal partnership. Dominance destroys peace in a home.

You already know that my marriage did not start out anything like a partnership. I was the dominant one. At that time, Karen's low self-esteem fully enabled my controlling, dominating ways. But she ultimately began to chafe under them.

In our case, I was the dominant figure; but dominance is as common among women as it is among men. Usually, when the wife is dominant, her husband has passive tendencies. That's because people always marry to their level of emotional health. If you marry someone who is very passive, very quiet and very tolerant, chances are you are a very dominant person. The challenge this presents is that you never respect the person you dominate; and the person who is dominated never respects the dominating mate.

The only hope for happiness in such a relationship is for the dominant person to give respect, esteem and some control to the person being dominated. And the person being dominated must stand up, be honest and enter fully into the relationship. Apathy and withdrawal on the part of a man exaggerates a wife's sense of insecurity and her temptation to be dominant.

On the other hand, when a man is allowed to get away with dominance by his wife—without her standing up in a loving way and asking to be treated with respect—it only encourages him in his dominance. Both sides have to work toward equality. The person beaten down has to assert her (his) will and the strength of her (his) personality to stand up and speak the truth; and the one who has been dominating has to submit himself (herself). That is how peace is achieved.

You will never find peace in marriage until you are equal partners—until you decide that you're going to discuss everything and you're not going to make a decision unless you make it together.

Karen and I make collaborative decisions. Part of our vision retreat each year is to sit down and ask each other, "What are we going to do concerning our finances?" On one occasion when we did this, Karen needed a new car, but we also desired to give some money to a special project at our church. We discussed where our priorities were and mutually decided we would give the money and wait on buying the car. During our discussion, I said, "Karen, I'm concerned about you and your car. I really want you to have a new car, but we want to pay cash for it." As the conversation ended, we were in complete agreement in our values, goals and decision concerning the car. There was no stress in our relationship, because we made the decision together.

The bottom line is that I don't bully her and she doesn't bully me.

When John Gottman did his study on shared control in relationships, he found that the ability to influence your spouse creates shared control; but refusal to receive influence creates division and, ultimately, a lack of satisfaction in the marriage.[2] If you're going to have peace in your marriage, you must be an equal partner. And you must be willing to be influenced.

Not dominated, influenced.

If you feel as if you're the one who is being dominated, don't be unrighteous or ungodly in your responses. It's possible to stand up for yourself and still be a redeemer. But don't allow yourself to be dominated either. In a loving way, say to your spouse, "I'm an equal here and I want to be heard. I don't want you making financial decisions without me. I don't want you making decisions concerning the kids without me. I don't want you making the decision about where we go to church and who we spend time with without me. I want to be heard." In other words, the spouse who has been dominating needs to be appropriately challenged.

People remain destructive—whether through drugs, alcohol or abuse—because they have enablers around them. What stops their abusive or destructive behavior is having someone who cares about them challenge them. They need someone who cares about them to stand up in a righteous way.

Our marriage changed the day Karen started standing up to me in our relationship. Let me tell you, when Karen began to lovingly but firmly confront my dominance, it shook my world. It forced me to make a decision about what I was going to do. In my case, I had a redeemer wife who had been praying for me, and I turned toward the Lord.

The person who has taken the dominant position has to make a decision that says, "Sure, I can be the ruler of my own little world, but it's lonely at the top. I can choose to continue being dominant, but I can't do that and share a partnership in which my spouse is happy and my home is filled with peace. I must treat this other person with respect." In other words, you have to be partners in the relationship.

This doesn't mean there can never be any decisions you make on your own. (Karen doesn't call me from the grocery store to get agreement on whether to buy Charmin or Cottonelle.) But major decisions should be made together. This means deciding together how you will discipline and educate your children and what values you will teach them, what you're going to do with your money, how you're going to give, how you're going to do church, how you will relate to your friends, and other decisions that affect the life you share.

Don't assume that what you're doing is right and that your spouse agrees. Sit down, talk it through and make sure you are partners. When you do that together—when you're partners in the enterprise of life—you will not be constantly sabotaging each other along the way. When you're partners in life and you've decided everything together, your journey will be a peaceful one.

THE FOURTH FOUNDATION: PRAYER

The fourth foundation of peace is *prayer*. Philippians 4:6-7 gives us some great instruction: "Be anxious for nothing, but in everything by prayer and supplication, with thanksgiving, let your requests be made known to God; and the peace of God, which surpasses all understanding, will guard your hearts and minds through Christ Jesus."

Peace that passes all understanding—being anxious for nothing. There's a strong thread running through this passage. Anxiety and stress come into your home and stay there when issues are in *your* hands—not God's. When stress and anxiety come into your home, it's a cue to pray.

Karen and I have prayed together for many years. When our kids were young, we used to walk in our neighborhood for an hour every morning. We would talk for 30 minutes and pray for 30 minutes. This was a foundational time in our marriage for making us one together in spirit. We prayed together, and together we saw answered prayer time after time. When we talked for 30 minutes, we would discover certain levels of anxiety related to kids, money, schedules and things like that. But 30 minutes of prayer totally defused the anxiety and restored peace in our relationship.

Often husbands need special help arriving at a place where they are comfortable praying with their wives. For a man, there can be a level of embarrassment or self-consciousness associated with praying with his wife. One reason for this is that men are emotionally modest. Women, on the other hand, tend to be emotionally immodest. A man's emotional modesty can make it hard for him to open up and pray with his wife.

Another common reason that men have difficulty praying with their wives is pride. When we pray, we are vulnerable. We have to humble ourselves. When we pray, we express dependence on God. We are being open about our weakness before God in prayer. For a man, this exposes a vulnerable side to his wife that she may have never seen before. That's certainly the way I felt when Karen first asked me to pray with her. I was embarrassed about it and just didn't know how to do it. It was a hard thing for me. But it's been one of the greatest blessings of my life.

A third major obstacle for many men stems from the way the concept of manhood has been twisted and distorted in our culture. The devil actually wants men to be proud of sin and embarrassed by righteousness; it should be the other way around! Take for example, a bunch of guys gathered around someone who is bragging about his latest sexual conquest and slapping him on the back. When a guy comes up and talks about taking his family to church, he gets mocked. That's an upside-down value system. A real man should be ashamed of sin and never ashamed of God.

As a man, you need to be the priest of your home. To do that, you have to break the ice. If you've never prayed with your wife, it's awkward when you first pray with her. But when you begin to pray with each other, it creates the deepest bond that can happen in a marriage relationship.

"Be anxious for nothing, but in everything by prayer and supplication, with thanksgiving, let your requests be made known to God; *and the peace of God, which surpasses all understanding.*" That last part simply means that you can't explain in natural terms *why* you feel so peaceful—you may have financial challenges, you may have personal challenges, but you have peace of mind. Why is this? Because both of you have invited God into your marriage. Jesus says, "If two of you agree on earth concerning anything that they ask, it will be done for them by My Father in heaven" (Matt. 18:19).

In 20 years of counseling, I have never once had a couple that prayed together come to me with a serious marriage problem. *Not once.* Invariably, the serious issues were in marriages in which there was no partnership of prayer. In other words, the marriages in trouble were the marriages in which God was excluded from the formula. And when you fail to include God through prayer, there can be no peace. Instead of peace, you feel panic because the only thing you have is what you can see, and you don't have enough of that. So it breeds a life of constant fear and anxiety.

When you are consistently coming together and asking Him to partner in your relationship—when you see God answering prayer after prayer, it brings peace. It assures you that you have financial resources beyond what you can see. You become intimately acquainted with, and confident in, a God in heaven who can supply all your needs beyond your ability to supply them yourself.

God honors a prayer of agreement. When a couple comes together, joins hands and says, "God, we don't know how to solve this problem. We don't know how to get through this issue. We need your wisdom," I'm telling you, God hears those prayers. And as a result, peace infuses the relationship.

Yes, prayer is the fourth foundation of the peace that is necessary for your relational paradise to be complete. Now let me summarize and weave these four elements together.

Peace in Paradise

In America today, when we're looking to complete the picture of paradise in marriage, peace is most often the missing element. The reason it is missing is because most couples (1) never sit down and come into agreement prior to the issues; (2) haven't agreed together before they start walking; (3) do not understand God's greater purpose for their lives; and (4) never take each other (and God) by the hand and pray together.

You see, it wasn't just Adam and Eve in paradise—it was Adam and Eve *and God.* God never intended for you to be in paradise without Him. When you're in paradise—the paradise of marriage—God is there as your partner. He's there to help you.

I challenge you to put God in the middle of your marriage. If you do, you'll find the missing element of peace begin to fill your souls and your home. When that happens, the result is a marriage that is on the way to being the paradise God wants it to be.

Notes

1. Jhodi Redlich, "Researchers Say 'Active Listening' Won't Keep Couples Tuned-in for a Happy Marriage," *Journal of Marriage and the Family,* February 20, 1998. http://www.gottman.com/press/releases/detail.php?id=13 (accessed February 2006).
2. Ibid.

CHAPTER 21

Living in Paradise

Marriage was God's idea. He blessed Adam and Eve with marriage and placed them in a perfect paradise. And when God looked at everything He had made (including a newly wed couple), He pronounced it "very good."

> Then God blessed them, and God said to them, "Be fruitful and multiply; fill the earth and subdue it; have dominion over the fish of the sea, over the birds of the air, and over every living thing that moves on the earth." And God said, "See, I have given you every herb that yields seed which is on the face of all the earth, and every tree whose fruit yields seed; to you it shall be for food. Also, to every beast of the earth, to every bird of the air, and to everything that creeps on the earth, in which there is life, I have given every green herb for food"; and it was so. Then God saw everything that He had made, and indeed it was very good (Gen. 1:28-31).

The word "blessed" in this passage means "to endue with power for success, prosperity, fertility and longevity." When God blessed Adam and Eve, His Spirit came upon them and empowered them to succeed in every area. God was an active participant in their lives. As long as they followed His pattern in their marriage, they experienced great blessing. Their marriage was *very good!*

However, when Adam and Eve rejected God's involvement and made decisions apart from His will, they moved out from under His blessing and experienced a curse instead.

The same thing happens in marriages today. It's easy to see that some marriages are wonderfully blessed while others are miserable. This isn't because God has favorites. God is no respecter of persons. It's due to the fact that some couples are following God's pattern for marriage, while others aren't. Some are living under God's blessing; others are living under the curse.

Really, it's a choice. God can and will bless you and your spouse—He desires to do just that. However, every blessing in the Bible is conditional. His blessings come through obedience.

Paradise for your marriage is a place of blessing, and here are three things you need to know about living the blessed life in paradise.

IT'S A SPIRITUAL THING

To begin with, you must recognize that marriage is a spiritual union that requires faith for success. Blessing emanates from the unseen spiritual realm—from God. Although many people view marriage as merely a legal or social institution, it isn't. Jesus made that clear when He said, "For this reason a man shall leave his father and mother and be joined to his wife, and the two shall become one flesh. So then, they are no longer two but one flesh. Therefore what God has joined together, let not man separate" (Matt. 19:5-6).

God spiritually joins a man and a woman together in marriage. It is first of all a spiritual relationship. And when God is involved, you're in a position to be blessed.

In the Garden of Eden, as long as Adam and Eve stayed in fellowship with God, they were at peace with each other and were blessed in their lives. But when they traded what God had given them for something He had forbidden, their marriage became cursed. The Spirit of God departed from them, and they were naked, afraid, divided, condemned and alone.

In order for you and your spouse to experience unity in your marriage, you must live by faith and you must value what God has given you. Live your lives as if God is present with you every minute—because He is!

You can't experience true intimacy apart from God. Why? Because the deepest part of you—your spirit—is where intimacy occurs. When you begin to honor marriage as a spiritual relationship, true intimacy will occur. Only when you and your wife are focused on spiritual things—praying together, worshiping God together—will you experience true fulfillment.

Jesus said, "Seek first the kingdom of God and His righteousness, and all these things shall be added to you" (Matt. 6:33). All things—the financial, social, physical and spiritual aspects of your life will be blessed when you seek God and allow Him to participate in your marriage.

So, men, even if it throws you out of your comfort zone, begin praying with your spouse. Go to church and worship God together. Read the Bible and talk about spiritual things. It will change your marriage. It will change your lives!

PARADISE HAS A KING

The second condition to living in paradise is recognizing God's authority in your marriage. He created marriage and He has all rights where your marriage is concerned. Remember, Adam and Eve lost the blessing of God when *they* took control.

Fix in your mind the fact that you don't own anything, not even your own body. Psalm 24:1 (*NIV*) tells us, "The earth is the LORD'S, and everything in it, the world and all who live in it." You are not your own; you were bought at a price—the precious blood of Jesus (see 1 Cor. 6:19-20). In the kingdom of God, you have no right to go your own way. Your decisions, your conduct, your marriage belong to God and His will. He knows what's best, and He wants your marriage to thrive!

For two people to live in peace, their wills must be submitted to one will—to God's. Recognizing and yielding to God's authority in your marriage will usher in unity and the blessings of God.

A PLACE OF PURPOSE

Finally, to walk in the fullness of God's blessings, you must understand His purpose for your marriage. God created you with an individual purpose, but He also created your marriage with a purpose. Adam and Eve were told to "be fruitful and multiply; fill the earth and subdue it" (Gen. 1:28). They were to take dominion over the earth. That was their purpose and they were blessed until they aborted God's mission in favor of their own plan.

God's common purpose for all marriages is:

- *Kingdom expansion*—people are redeemed and the Church is established.
- *Image expression*—we are God's image bearers to our children, and our marriages are to be an expression of the love of Jesus to the world.
- *Character preservation*—by loving each other, we will stay out of sin. In 1 Peter 3, we learn that if a husband doesn't love his wife properly, God will not hear his prayers.

By having a common purpose, you and your mate can be a blessing to others. As you respect the spiritual nature of marriage, and as you recognize God's authority and fulfill God's purpose in your marriage, the blessings of God will become evident in every area of your life.

Start Your Journey

Together we have explored the seven secrets that unfailingly lead to a paradise-on-Earth marriage. My prayer is that by now a spark of hope has been kindled in your soul—hope that your marriage can be stronger, healthier and more fulfilling than it is today—and that you have a vision for something far better than you are experiencing right now.

I believe with all my heart that any couple that applies the principles I've outlined in this book, and will look to and lean on God for grace, wisdom and strength, will find their relationship on a path to wholeness and blessing.

Karen and I have seen this happen in our home. And in the years since we first began teaching God's way to wholeness and blessing in marriage, we've seen the same thing transform the homes of countless other couples as well.

Be encouraged. Although your journey won't be easy, it will be worth the effort.

Oh yes—it's worth it!

Prayer, Partnership and Purpose

If you want to experience a life-time of paradise, walk together in agreement as equal partners and understand that there is a greater purpose for your marriage than just living for yourselves, prayer, partnership and purpose will bring you to your secret paradise.

The Path to Paradise

I want to close with a prayer of blessing for your marriage relationship. I have prayed similar prayers many times, at the close of marriage seminars and counseling sessions. Now I pray these things for you.

Holy Spirit, You are the Spirit of joy. You are the Spirit of peace. You are the Spirit of long-suffering. That's why I'm asking You right now to enter the marriage of the person holding this book. Give this person and spouse the wisdom to do the right thing to resolve the issues that are pulling them apart. Lord, I'm asking You to give them a purpose for their marriage that is bigger than they are—a purpose that is part of the bigger story of what You are doing in the world today.

I pray that when they try to find a reason to stay together they will find it easily. I'm asking You, Holy Spirit, to give them vision for their future and an answer to why You have put them together—that when someone asks them the question, What is your marriage about? they will know. I'm asking You, Lord, to bless this couple so precious to You. I'm asking that You would open the windows of heaven and pour out Your blessings on them. Grant their hearts' desire and give them such fulfillment, such blessing together, that they will live in a paradise of marriage for the rest of their lives. In Jesus' name, amen.

The Heart of Paradise
Keeping Passion in Your Marriage

During the course of more than 20 years of helping married couples, Karen and I have seen firsthand how important are the intangible elements—intimacy, romance, passion—to maintaining a strong, satisfying marriage.

Once you arrive at your own secret paradise, you will have to know the secrets of cultivating romance if you want to remain there. Those secrets aren't the same for men and women. As we saw throughout the pages of *Our Secret Paradise*, husbands and wives are wired very differently, but both men and women share a very fundamental hunger for intimacy and passion.

With that in mind, allow me to share some of the keys to keeping the fires of romance stoked in your marriage—speaking first to men and then to women.

FOR HUSBANDS

What does it mean to be romantic toward your wife? What does romance look like? Many men simply don't know how to answer those questions. Perhaps giving your wife flowers and chocolates once a year is your idea of fulfilling your role of being romantic. If so, you wouldn't be alone. Many men tend to associate the idea of romance solely with Valentine's Day. They take a stab at "romance" once a year, not realizing the benefits of creating romance in their marriages on a regular basis.

The benefits of creating romance in your marriage far outweigh the effort. In fact, adding romance is not that difficult to do. While it's true that romance and passion don't happen automatically, it's also true that you have the power to create romance and passion at any time. That's right. Once you understand the *chemistry of romance,* you will understand how to create and sustain passion and romance in your relationship for a lifetime.

In fact, romance is a *decision* that creates a passionate atmosphere in your marriage relationship.

You begin to put passion in your marriage by first *deciding* to be a romantic husband. And to set the record straight, romance isn't just for a select few who happen to have a naturally romantic personality. Nor is it relegated to strange men and silly women.

Romance is the cornerstone of any healthy marriage relationship because God made us that way.

Intuitive Versus Educated Romance

First, it's important to recognize that there are two types of romance. The first type can be described as *intuitive romance.* Allow me to explain. When you met your wife and fell in love with her, creating romance probably wasn't a problem. You didn't have to think about it, did you? You were keenly interested in her and wanted her to be keenly interested in you, so you instinctively did things to please her.

Remember the days of washing your car before every date? Opening doors, giving her flowers and always putting your best foot forward? You wanted to spend time with her, so you made time for her. She was the focus of your attention and affection while you were pursuing her.

I imagine that she felt and acted the same way toward you, right? You were cultivating and enjoying intuitive romance.

So, what happens after we get married? Sadly, many of us don't really expect to have a marriage that continues to experience real passion through the years. Few of us saw it in our parents' marriages. And we're often reminded that once the kids come along, when job pressures build and the task of running a home looms large, we just won't have the time and energy to keep the love alive in our marriages.

That seems to be the norm. *It's okay,* we tell ourselves. *The honeymoon can't last forever.* If you buy into that thinking, then you're buying into a lie!

If you're like most couples, after you got married and the honeymoon was "over," you forgot all about creating romance in your relationship. No longer did you need to capture her heart, because you had it now! Your life settled into a routine. The passion you once had together was gradually replaced by a comfortable taking each other for granted.

In essence, intuitive romance dissipates in your relationship. However, that doesn't mean romance has to die. There's another kind of romance that is just as effective and exciting as the intuitive kind. It's called *educated romance.*

In fact, educated romance is the best kind of romance, because it can be cultivated and enjoyed for the rest of your life. It isn't something you do for a few weeks or months. The practice of educated romance will enable you to build and sustain a truly great marriage. But you'll need a little chemistry lesson. First you need to understand the three basic elements of romance.

First Element of Romance: Meeting an Unspoken Need

"I'm just in a romantic *mood* tonight."

Have you ever said something similar to those words?

Well, I have news for you. Contrary to popular belief, romance is not a feeling or a mood that just can't be controlled. Rather, it's an atmosphere that must be created. There are basically three chemical elements of romance. When these elements come together, the sparks will fly in a good way! You will experience a little bit of heaven right here on Earth.

The first element in creating romance is *meeting an unspoken need.*

You initiate romance. Your wife should not have to keep telling you what she likes or doesn't like, what her desires are, etc. (In fact, if she has to ask or hint, it's by definition *not* romantic.) You should make it your business to know what is important to her. That means you buy flowers and give them to your wife before she mentions that it's her birthday!

Think back to when you first fell in love with your wife. Remember how you spent massive amounts of time studying her? You were determined to get a Ph.D. in her—in loving your sweetheart. You tried to anticipate what you could do to please her. You desired to be with her every day, all day. Your actions indicated that she was on your heart and mind, and you wanted to bless her in some way. When you were dating your wife, she knew that you would not be her dream breaker; rather, she saw you as her dream maker.

That's romance!

She did the same for you, no doubt. Didn't you love the way she made you feel? Didn't you love how she believed in you? Didn't she make you feel capable, special and unique?

There were two vital components to your relationship. The first was made up of your feelings for your wife—the reasons why you fell in love with her. The second was made up of the way she made you feel about yourself—how she made you feel important and desirable.

You can see how your love during courtship was broken up into two aspects. You can also see how the language of desire drew you and your wife closer together. Every person wants to know that she (or he) is desirable.

When you initiate romance in your marriage relationship, you communicate to your wife that she is desirable to you. How do you start adding romance? You do what you did when you were dating. Study your wife. Notice what kinds of jewelry or perfume she likes. Make a note when she comments about the things she would like to have or like to do. Pay attention to her and to her desires. Then meet those desires in unexpected ways.

Second Element of Romance: Speaking Your Wife's Love Language

If you, like many men, have no problem agreeing that your wife speaks an entirely different love language than you do, then it's important that you learn to communicate in your wife's language. You can begin by understanding her four primary needs.

1. *Your wife needs to feel secure.* You can help her feel secure by being selfless and sacrificial.
2. *Your wife needs open and honest communication with you.* Don't talk to her in one-line sentences. Or, as I always say, "Don't give her

the headlines when she wants to suck your brain out." Recognize that your wife has an unspoken mission to put you in touch with your emotions. Not only will this make her happy, but you will also benefit from and learn to enjoy the experience.

3. *Your wife craves soft, nonsexual affection.* This type of affection makes her feel cherished, valuable and safe, which in turn paves the way for her to become aroused. So take note of this fact: The more soft and nonsexual you are toward your wife, the more sexual she will become.

4. *Your wife needs for you to be a good leader.* This doesn't mean she wants to be dominated. She needs for you to be the loving initiator in finances, in creating a spiritual atmosphere in your home, in being involved with the children, and in creating romance.

Communicating with your wife in these ways will cause her to be drawn to you. She will in turn desire to bless you. As you sow these things into her life, you will reap a harvest in your own.

Keep in mind that the chemistry of romance begins when you and she first get out of bed in the morning. Her life, probably unlike yours— is a continuum. All things are connected—every event, relationship, kid, finances, and so forth affect her as a whole. So don't think that the minute you get home from work she's going to be ready to get intimate with you. Things must be in order before she can relax and enjoy the experience.

A romantic night to her will likely mean candlelight; a long meal with a lot of talking; slow, nonsexual touch; the expression of emotion. Sex is the last thing on her mind when she thinks of romance. Although this may initially seem grueling, it will be well worth the effort in the end! I know this is true because I've proven it in my own life.

Once I began to talk to Karen, to be affectionate with her and to give her what she needed, I learned to enjoy talking almost as much as she does. She's put me in touch with a world I didn't know existed. Her world is a world I've learned to love, and she has learned to love mine.

So don't wait any longer to learn to speak your wife's love language on a regular basis. It's part of the chemistry of romance. Happiness, goodwill and met needs will be the result!

Third Element of Romance: Communicating Unique Value to Your Wife

The third element of romance is communicating *unique* value to your wife. Romance is reserved for one person and one person alone—for the one to whom you are married. Romance is a unique language that communicates value to that one unique individual.

Invariably, a marriage begins to go bad when a wife or husband no longer feels valued. Communicating value to your spouse takes consistency. It takes filling your wife's heart with positive words. Praise her. Make it a point every day to tell her how much you value and appreciate her.

You can also show your wife how valuable she is through what is called *comparative value*. What you are willing to give up for her shows her how much you think she is worth. For instance, are you willing to give up time at the office to spend time with her? Are you willing to forego a Saturday morning tee-time with the guys to take her to breakfast?

You can also communicate value to your wife by simply having a great attitude toward her. At times that kind of attitude includes giving to your wife sacrificially and serving her. Giving her gifts can make a huge deposit in the bank of romance. Even though your relationship isn't based on material things, you can communicate how you value her by giving her things of value.

You may have to sacrifice something you want to purchase in order to buy something meaningful for her. This kind of gift says, "You mean more to me than anybody else on Earth. You are uniquely valuable to me."

Creative energy—such as writing her a poem or some other written expression—is a way to communicate value. There is no end to the possible ways you can communicate to your wife how you value, love and cherish her.

Remember, romance is a *decision* to create a passionate atmosphere in your marriage relationship. You hold the key to romance—now go unlock your wife's heart and step into a little bit of heaven on Earth!

FOR WIVES

Romance is something few people truly understand. Yet it's something every little girl dreams of and every woman longs for.

Romance, however, is not just for women. Men also crave romance. Although you may not think so at times, deep down, your husband longs for you to be romantic toward him. He needs to know that you desire him.

Creating romance in your relationship is vitally important. It's the cornerstone to every blessed marriage. The good news is that romance toward your husband is within your grasp today. I say that because romance isn't something reserved for the favored few who marry that "right man" with a romantic bent.

No. Romance happens at *your* discretion. That's right, dear lady. Romance is a *decision* you can make that will create a passionate atmosphere in your marriage relationship.

For the most part, neither passion nor romance will occur automatically—you create them with the three elements of the chemistry of romance:

1. Meeting your husband's unspoken needs.
2. Speaking your spouse's love language.
3. Communicating unique value to your husband.

Each of these elements is important. Through romance, you communicate to your husband his desirability. He needs to know that you desire him and him alone. Romance was the emotional cornerstone of why you fell in love in the first place and it remains the emotional cornerstone for passion and intimacy. Every couple is looking for passion and intimacy—the prizes at the end of the romantic trail.

Romance also builds the relationship skills you need in marriage. When you're not actively being romantic, those skills diminish, which can cause the relationship to weaken.

Being actively romantic also closes the door to temptation. The devil is always looking for a way to tempt us to go outside of our marriage relationship to get our needs met. But when romance is alive and well in a marriage, the door of temptation gets slammed shut.

Understanding Your Husband's Needs

God gave you and your husband energy to love one another. But most couples use this energy to try to change each other. A lot of men are just looking for a physical female with an emotional male inside. Many women are looking for a physical male with an emotional female inside. If you're married to an average male, you need to know that he's different from you in profound ways.

That is because God did not create men and women to match each other; He created men and women to complement each other. Men and women are different physically and emotionally. Their needs are different. The wonderful thing about romance is that it can bring the two worlds together, and you can both gain access to a world you never knew existed. So make it a point to understand your husband and his world. Make it a point to meet his needs. As a result, your needs will be met too.

The Chemistry of Romance Includes Honor

The number one need for a man is to receive honor.

Men are as sensitive in their egos as women are physically sensitive. That's easy to see when I look at my wife and my daughter, who are so gentle physically, as opposed to my son who is 6'4" and would probably pin me in seconds in a wrestling match! You know that men are tough physically, but just the slightest word of dishonor from a woman is devastating to a man.

Ladies, do yourself a favor and learn this truth: Men gravitate to praise and they distance themselves from dishonor.

Your husband has a profound need for you to honor and respect him. Creating the chemistry of romance in your marriage begins with honor. Recognize and appreciate his strengths. Don't always point out his weaknesses.

The Chemistry of Romance Includes Sex

Sexual intimacy is a primary need for a man. Say the word "romance" to a man and he hears the word "sex." When men are asked to list how important sex is to them, they consistently rank it first or second, and occasionally third. Women, however, on average, list sex as thirteenth in importance—listing gardening in twelfth position!

In case you don't already know this, your husband is very visual. He wants to see your body. You may not want to see it, but he does. So let him. If you want the chemistry of romance working in your marriage, don't buy flannel; buy lingerie that your husband will like.

I was doing a marriage seminar one time in Pennsylvania, and I said, "Ladies, there is a place for flannel nightgowns." A male voice yelled out, "Yeah, the fireplace!" He was right.

Burn the flannel pajamas!

The Chemistry of Romance Includes Kindred Fellowship

The third need men have is for kindred fellowship. Your husband wants to have fun with you. He wants you to be his friend. That's the way he fell in love with you, isn't it? Remember how you did things to please him? Remember how you wanted to spend time with him, so you made time for him? If he went fishing, you tagged along. If he wanted to watch the ballgame, you fixed him popcorn and a Coke and snuggled on the couch beside him. No matter what he was doing, you wanted to be with him, right?

He was the focus of your attention and affection while you were dating.

If you're like most couples, after you got married and the honeymoon period was over, you forgot all about creating romance in your relationship. No longer did you need to capture his heart, because you had it. Your life settled into a routine. Taking each other for granted replaced the passion to be together.

Your husband still needs for you to be his buddy—his best friend. Having fun with him will meet one of his greatest needs. When you have children, this planning takes effort. Not only can finding the time and a babysitter be an issue, but also many women fall into the trap of mothering their husbands. They become absorbed in the identity of being a mother and it bleeds over into the marriage relationship. This behavior is a romance robber!

Don't mother your husband. Be his best friend. Make time to do things he likes to do and you will create the chemistry of romance in your relationship.

Learn to Speak "Man"

Finally, *it's important that you communicate in a romantic language that your husband can understand.*

To a woman, a romantic evening is a wonderful meal, candlelight and Luther Vandross music. In an effort to teach her husband about romance, she might say, "I want a romantic evening, and here's what is going to happen. We're going to keep our clothes on for a long time and just touch and kiss in a nonsexual way. We're going to get in touch with our emotions and we're going to have a really nice evening. We're not going to have sex for a very long time, if at all."

The problem with this scenario is that she's not speaking his language; she's speaking hers. She's giving him a language lesson about her language rather than communicating in a language that he can understand. He's on the other side of the table saying, "No speaky *woman*!" She can tell he's not getting it. It's not meeting his need. And both of them become totally frustrated from the experience.

Every healthy marriage must be emotionally bilingual.

When a man is being romantic with his wife, he should not be trying to gulp down a sandwich while he tries to rip off her clothes and drag her into the bedroom to watch ESPN while having sex. Although that's "romantic" for a man, it isn't for a woman.

If you want to create romance for your husband, gear the whole evening around what he likes to do. When he comes home from work, make sure the house is in order and the kids are at the sitter's house. Greet him at the door in a sexy negligee. When he walks in, say to him, "You're the greatest man on Earth." Kiss him passionately. Make him feel like he's desirable. Praise him. Have quick finger foods prepared and sitting next to the bed. Say to him, "You are so wonderful. What can I do for you? I'm here to serve you." Have sex with him.

After you pick him up off the floor, he'll say, "You're the best woman on Earth. I love you so much!"

If you speak your husband's language and meet his needs, you will develop a closer connection with him. Your relationship will be strengthened. Passion and romance will be ignited in your marriage.

Go to School and Study Your Husband

The bottom line is that romance takes time and effort. It is as much discipline as it is emotion. Begin to educate yourself on what your husband's needs are, and then discipline yourself to meet those needs. You can fall back in love through educated romance. You can create passion and intimacy by practicing the chemistry of romance.

It's a decision. You can make it happen. The more meaningful romance is not the *instinctive* romance of the courtship days. The more meaningful romance is the *educated* romance that is born of selflessness, choice and discipline. From this day forward you can love your husband in a certain way that will create an atmosphere of romance. It's not a matter of luck and it's not a matter of fate. It's something that you can make happen.

You can become attuned to what your partner likes. It's fun to be creative in how you meet your partner's needs. You don't have to let your marriage become boring. Ask the Lord to give you ideas about how you can bless your husband. Find out what interests him and educate yourself in these matters. Then talk with him about those things.

When you and your husband fell in love, more than likely, you were very energetic and you worked hard at loving each other and meeting each other's needs. When that kind of creativity and energy stops, the romance stops.

Don't allow children to get in the way of keeping your relationship alive. It's never too late to get back the romance. You can always get it back if you are willing to do the right thing regardless of what your spouse does. By turning up the thermostat on your side of the house, it will warm him up in a hurry.

You hold the lighter in your hand. Ignite that passion and romance beginning today!

CONCLUSION

God created us to be people of passion. Just as He is passionate about loving us, He designed us to be passionate about loving each other. This kind of passion has nothing to do with feelings; it is a daily decision—*Today, I will love my spouse as Christ loves me.*

God doesn't draw us to Himself and then leave us hanging. He is the same yesterday, today and tomorrow. Christ is our role model, not the dysfunctional couples on TV who can't get it right, and not our friends who know even less than we do.

To love your spouse like Christ loves the Church, think of what He does:

1. He loved us before we loved Him (see 1 John 4:19).
2. His love covers a multitude of sins (see 1 Pet. 4:8).
3. Nothing we do can separate us from His love (see Rom. 8:35-39).

Ultimately, it is this kind of unselfishness and care that will keep intimacy and passion alive in your marriage relationship for a lifetime.

About the Author

Jimmy Evans is one of America's leading authorities on family and marriage relationships. He is founder and president of *MarriageToday*™, a marriage ministry and nationally broadcast television program.

Jimmy's passion for marriage was born out of the pain and near failure of his own marriage with his wife, Karen. As they both began to study and seek God's help to turn around their troubled relationship, they began to learn key Biblical principles that allowed God to heal them and help them build a strong and happy marriage. Realizing that there was a great need in the Church to help other couples who were struggling in their marriages, Jimmy began to counsel couples and lead small group Bible studies in his and Karen's home. With an obvious anointing to minister to people with troubled marriages, Jimmy's influence and desire continued to grow over the next 22 years as he moved from small group leader to marriage counselor to Senior Pastor of Trinity Fellowship Church.

During this time, the *MarriageToday*™ ministry was born. Now in its twelfth year, *MarriageToday*™ is aired nationally to millions of homes each day. On this program, Jimmy and Karen share practical and biblical truths with viewers on how to build a strong and happy marriage. The format of the *MarriageToday*™ television program is warm and welcoming and is targeted toward a wide range of viewers. The program includes Jimmy's teachings as well as input from leading marriage and family experts from across the nation.

Jimmy has authored several books and has created many seminars and resource materials to help build and strengthen marriages. Some of his well-known works include *Marriage on the Rock, Freedom From Your Past, The Seven Secrets for Successful Families,* and *Resolving Stress in Your Marriage.* He is a popular church and conference speaker. Jimmy and Karen have been married for more than 32 years, and they have two married adult children and two granddaughters.

Thanks

Many people were involved in the process of writing this book. I want to specifically thank David Holland for his talent and help in putting the passion of my heart into written words. I also would like to thank Kim LaNore, Cory Albracht and Regal books for their encouragement and support for this effort. Your assistance in getting this work published was invaluable.

I especially want to thank my wife, Karen, for her undying love and support for me for more than 30 years. She has been my helpmate, my encourager and my best friend. Karen's prayers and commitment to me and to our marriage have been a catalyst to help get us through hard times and have enabled us to live out our own secret paradise.

MarriageToday™
Contact Information:

8101 Royal Ridge Parkway
Irving, TX 75063

P.O. Box 59888
Dallas, TX 75229

972-953-0500
www.marriagetoday.org

More Books That Offer
Big Help for Relationships